To 43,

This Blessed Plot

Hazel Southam.

This Blessed Plot

Hazel Southam

CANTERBURY
PRESS
Norwich

© Hazel Southam 2021

First published in 2021 by the Canterbury Press Norwich
Editorial office
3rd Floor, Invicta House
108–114 Golden Lane
London EC1Y 0TG, UK
www.canterburypress.co.uk

Canterbury Press is an imprint of Hymns Ancient & Modern Ltd
(a registered charity)

Hymns Ancient & Modern® is a registered trademark of
Hymns Ancient & Modern Ltd
13A Hellesdon Park Road, Norwich,
Norfolk NR6 5DR, UK

British Library Cataloguing in Publication data

A catalogue record for this book is available
from the British Library

ISBN 978-1-78622-342-5

Typeset by Regent Typesetting
Printed and bound by
CPI Group (UK) Ltd

This book is dedicated to Mary Southam,
who loved orchards.

Contents

Acknowledgements

My heart is full of gratitude to all the people who've made this adventure possible. Maurice McDonagh and Jim Meharg took the initiative and turned my dream into reality at the outset. After them, a whole community absorbed and helped me, so my thanks go to everyone at the allotments who's ever been kind, lent me their power tools, helped build something, passed on seeds, donated plants or offered words of encouragement. You know who you are. You are all special and much appreciated.

Particular thanks go to those who, through geography, ended up helping me more than they might have imagined was feasible: Barbara, Garry, James and James, Nikki, Allison, Kasia, Rose, Merv, Val, Gary, Fran, Ian, Mike and Pete.

None of this would have been possible without the encouragement of good friends: Laura Pritchard, Geordie Torr, Fran Clifton, Rachel Bassindale, Phil Comer and Sarah Eberle.

All these people, and more, have helped achieve something that seemed unreachable and beyond me, but that has been utterly enriching. Any success is theirs. Any mistakes in the telling are mine.

Thanks also go to the team at Hymns Ancient & Modern who thought that this was a tale worth telling. I hope it inspires you.

Preface

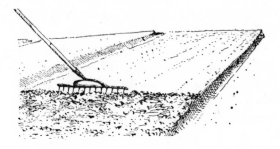

Come through the big metal gate into a hidden, little-seen world. Tucked away on the edge of Winchester lie the Highcliffe Allotments, snuggled between the M3 and a housing estate. It isn't glamorous, but it's a little slice of heaven that locals have been working for more than 100 years.

As you walk with me along the bumpy track, you'll see more than 100 plots, some tidy, some less so, all productive and special in their own way. The track is rutted and plots lie on either side. The M3 is to our right, the housing estate to our left. And at the end there are fields that are home to pigs, sheep, hens and geese.

We'll pass the goats on our left and say hello to a few friends on our way in, some of whose names have been changed in this book. Because the site is on the side of a hill (all of Winchester is on a hill) it's windy here, even on a still summer's day. The soil depends on where you are, and how much it's been worked. On my plot it's heavy, formerly unloved clay. But the good news is that the plot is south-facing, the great joy of gardeners, as it gives their plants the longest possible hours of sunlight.

When we've walked 100 yards, we come to two small plots on the right-hand side of the track in need of much love and attention. I have been assigned the lower one, so I am entirely surrounded by other allotments and can watch and learn from their development.

This is the story about the transformation of that plot and the unexpected transformation that it wrought in me. It's cheaper than therapy, and at the end there's something to eat, in fact lots to eat. I am not a world-famous gardener. I'm a middle-aged woman trying something new. I'm also a journalist, and have spent more than 30 years telling other people's stories, both in this country and around the world. It was a surprise to be grounded and have my own story changed by a small patch of earth, to find that patch of ground shaping and telling my story, revealing my weaknesses and strengths, opening a chink in my heart for renewal and the growth of faith as well as vegetables. I was only expecting lettuces, so that was a surprise.

Let me encourage you, if you've ever enjoyed a meal and wondered where your food came from, to try growing something. Growing connects us with our food, but also with the weather, seasons and the land that we inhabit. It reminds us of our mortality, and takes us beyond ourselves into community, spirituality and our place in the world. It is about a great deal more than vegetables, but the vegetables are enjoyable too.

Take a seat under the Victoria plum tree where there is some shade. You, like everyone else, are welcome here. Gardening like this is about growing friendships, as well as growing plants. It's about people and their stories. You can't be a solitary allotment holder. So, welcome to a small space of flourishing.

Introduction

Everything changed over a cup of tea. Perhaps as I'm English, that isn't surprising. Life revolves around tea. It was a chance conversation with my 91-year-old mother that swept in the change. Every now and then we have The Conversation about why I'm not married. Answer: the marriages I saw up close as a child were off-putting. Far, far too many compromises were being made by the women. There seemed to be more hurt and sadness than joy, contentment or simply even-handedness. I decided early on that marriage didn't appeal. Too late, I realized that there are better, healthier ways of being married than those early examples. But there's no way back, and I am content with my lot. The journalist's life has taken me around the UK and the world. I have kind friends and delightful god-children. You could do a lot worse.

And what are the options? Online dating? The very thought makes me shudder. So when The Conversation came around again, I searched for comparisons, for dreams that might actually be fulfilled. Even the idea of marriage, let alone the reality, is in the rear-view mirror. 'Honestly,' I said, 'I'd rather have an orchard than be married.'

As I said it, it became true. The words hung in the air, almost glistening. In that moment, planting fruit trees became what I wanted to do. I have no children as a legacy for my life, but an orchard would be a good second.

Both my mother and I seized upon the idea. We'd grown up, like generations of our family, in a village in Buckinghamshire. Back then, in the 1960s, the village was still full of the cherry orchards that had been its livelihood. The cherries went to market. The wood was turned into chair legs. My grandfather talked of picking cherries and putting them on the London train in the morning. My great-uncle was a bodger, turning chair legs for the nearby chair-making industry.

This isn't a far-off Arcadia. It's living memory of real lives. But the orchards are grubbed up now. New housing stands where they once blossomed. According to government statistics, half of Britain's pear orchards and two-thirds of its apple orchards have been felled since 1970. I can find no statistics for cherry orchards, which tells a story in itself.

In my grandparents' day, more than 200 varieties of fruit could be found growing in Britain's orchards, and each village had its own unique varieties. Our village, Holmer Green, was cherry central. My father recalled everything stopping for the cherry harvest: men, women and children picking the fruit for weeks, until it had all been harvested and sold. Enormous care was taken of the trees. Great pride attached to how long a ladder you could carry by yourself. Tireless wars were waged against starlings, the major threat to the harvest. If a flock of starlings landed in your trees, they could ruin the harvest in an hour. Keeping them out of the trees was the challenge.

My father's solution was The Clanger. Bits of old metal hung in a bunch from the bough of a cherry tree. Two ropes attached it to the sitting room and my parents' bedroom. When my father heard starlings he could pull the rope, even if he was in bed, and clang, the metal would fall into a metal wheel-barrow, the noise scattering the invading starlings.

Like all our neighbours, we had quite a bit of land, and it was stuffed with fruit trees. My sun-filled memories of child-hood are of joining my father in scaring the starlings out of the cherry trees and climbing traditional cherry ladders to pick basket after basket of fruit.

We had four main varieties in our garden. The Early River is a red-black variety that starts to fruit at the end of May, and dates back to 1872. It was followed by the Waterloo, one of the oldest known varieties in Britain, first planted here in 1815. It has luscious dark-red flesh and is thickly juicy.

Then came two Bigarreaux. Bigarreau Napoleon dates to 1832 and is a beautiful, large, yellow, heart-shaped fruit with a blush of pink. Then there's the Yellow Bigarreau, endemic, it seems, to our village, and barely found anywhere else now. It is what it says, a big, yellow, juicy, fleshy cherry, and my complete favourite.

Fruit was everywhere, and, if I wanted a snack, all I had to do was pick a greengage from the tree by the pond; or a few cherries from the huge trees by the house; or wander down to our own apple orchard. More hours were spent harvesting the raspberries while listening to *Test Match Special* on a portable radio that my father, an electronic engineer, had made out of spare parts.

There was a tree in our apple orchard with branches so low that a small child could sit on them without climbing. Sitting there, I was surrounded by trees: our apples and, behind our garden, an extensive orchard of plums and cherries. In spring, it was a frothy white-and-pinkness. Those low branches were where I went for a bit of peace, as from here I could see no man-made thing, not even our own home. However beautiful the setting, no life is perfect. Like any home, things were happening that weren't spoken of to a child, but the emotions were present, and I picked up on them. Some things were inexplicable, unknowable until much later. So, I would sit there until my own emotions softened and I could return to the fray of life and playing. As a six-year-old, it appears, I was an early practitioner of mindfulness.

I have been looking for an emotional equivalent of those branches ever since, and never quite found it. Suddenly, I realized that I could simply plant my own trees and create that environment, perhaps even experience that sense of restoration again. I would never sit on the low branches of the trees I planted. But a child of the future might. What better legacy could I leave? By planting an orchard (however small), I would be part of the continuum of my family who planted trees and harvested from them for many generations. It would also be a small act of defiance, a denial of today's society that uproots ancient woodlands to create faster train lines and builds houses on floodplains. And if I did it, could it also be an inspiration to others? After all, every garden, whatever its size, can accommodate a fruit tree. Perhaps it should be mandatory.

For months I scoured sales for woodland. It wasn't quite what I was after, but it might do. It might. But I never saw anything under £45,000, and generally the asking price was £10,000–30,000 more than this. By emptying out all my pockets and looking under the sofa, I had nothing near this.

It was time to reconsider. So it was that one fateful day in 2018, I mentioned my fruitless search to Maurice, the front-of-house manager at the hairdresser's. He had an allotment. I thought it might be a subject of interest while I waited to get my hair cut. That was all.

'You can plant trees at our allotments,' he said. 'I'll ring the site manager.'

Two days later the phone rang. It was the site manager. The plot next to his was a shocking mess. But it had a plum, an apple and a pear tree. I danced with joy. I was on my way to having an orchard and at least some of my dreams would be fulfilled. In fact, during the following year, there'd be a lot more than that.

JANUARY

Preparation

On the highest branch of a bare, winter plum tree, a robin is singing. Clear, trilling, confident notes tumble around me. I stop digging and enjoy the performance. It is 14 degrees in the sunshine. It feels like spring, not January. And I am digging up worms. He has something to sing about.

Behind the robin's song is the sound of bells, ringing in the new year. The bell-ringers of Winchester are doing this on a grand scale, as the peal pours and tumbles along the slope all morning, echoing the robin's joy.

The robin sings to maintain his territory and attract a mate. The bell ringers are celebrating the new year. And I am digging because I'm creating something new: my first allotment. By this stage, I've had the allotment for six months, most of which has been spent hacking back undergrowth, finding the ground and then planting a few vegetables in it as a token gesture. This is my first full growing year, the year when the reality of working this plot will take shape. What I don't realize yet is that I'm also creating a new way of life, one that enables me to be much more closely in touch with nature, the seasons, the earth, the weather, and through all of this, with myself, my food, my community and, unexpectedly, my faith. This isn't just new year, this is new everything. Increasingly, we're realizing the links between gardening (let's include tending an allotment in that) and good mental health and well-being as well as physical health. This is about to become a reality for me.

But for now, today is about digging. Before I can eat, I must harvest. Before I harvest, I must nurture. Before I nurture, I must sow. And before I sow, I must dig. January is not just about digging. It is about planning. However enthusiastic you are, however many sets of wet-weather clothes you have, the days are short in January and it is sometimes hard to prise yourself off the sofa, away from the fire, and outdoors. So, January is about preparation: preparing the soil for the year ahead; preparing the plot by giving it shape and structure; preparing for what I will grow; and preparing myself for a new adventure: a quiet adventure that is the very stuff of life.

In a must-have, need-it-now society, it can be easy to fall into the trap of thinking that immediacy is good. It is if it's vital healthcare. For everything else, immediacy takes away the twin joys of planning and looking forward to something.

Think about your holiday, or your birthday. Much of the pleasure gained from it is in the months or weeks spent dreaming about it ahead of time. Growing your own food is the same. I could go to the supermarket and take vegetables off the shelf, but where would be the pleasure in that? I would have no involvement in the food that I'm eating. By planning the plot, improving the soil, working with what I have, and spending months nurturing, I'm completely invested in the meals that I eat and the land that I'm part of. I'll have meaningful food and the pleasure of growing it.

Growing your own fruit and vegetables on an allotment is now so popular that frequently, around the country, there are waiting lists to get a plot. According to the National Allotment Society, across Britain an estimated 90,000 people are queuing for an allotment, with some of them having to wait up to 40 years for a plot. That's longer than getting into the MCC or signing your child up for Eton, though I grant you that the £25 annual fee I pay is less expensive. How long you have to wait depends on where you live. It is a postcode lottery.

I was lucky. It took just two days before my half-formed dream of planting fruit trees became a reality and an allotment was mine, the dream of having an orchard on its way to being realized.

It doesn't take much to be an orchard. Just five trees constitute one. But what a difference those trees make. That environment is often a haven for bats, badgers, owls and woodpeckers, as well as any number of pollinators.

One of the happiest experiences of my childhood was sitting watching the fading light of a May evening from my bedroom windowsill. Everything was still, violet, pink and gold, and the garden was alive with pipistrelle bats who swept in every evening to feed on the insects drawn to the fruit trees.

Perhaps I could recreate this, in miniature? Badgers were unlikely to venture into an allotment, especially given that our site lies less than a mile from the M3, but bats and pollinators surely would. Once again I would have the pleasure of picking fruit from the tree, rather than buying it, wrapped in endless plastic. The die was cast.

There is an old Chinese saying that the best time to plant a tree was 20 years ago. The second-best time is today. The allotments' rules state that plots work on a rule of thirds: no more than a third of a plot can be given over to anything, including trees. They have to be on dwarf rooting stock so that they don't grow too high and shade your neighbour's vegetables. It's only polite.

Despite these constraints, I can have an orchard. And, if I'm having an orchard, I want to be inventive. So, in the weeks before this pivotal year, I opted for three Hampshire heritage varieties of apple; a greengage (to remind me of my childhood); and a quince, which are to be espaliered along the fence-lines of the plot. They were planted one sunny December day and even now, a month later in January, I can barely believe they are there. I have seven trees in all: technically an orchard even if it doesn't look like one. It's not a patch on my childhood, but it is so much better than nothing. And I can wait to see them grow and flourish.

It's testament to the fact that, if you want to change a situation, you can. All it takes is the will and a bit of hard graft. Every garden really can have a tree. No matter how small your plot, even if it's just a pot or container, a tree can be had. Trees change everything. They put our lives into perspective. They create habitat, and they are the lungs of the world.

But, rather like dusting, or perhaps ironing, planting a tree is one of those things we'll do 'one day'. 'One day' never comes. The planet's lungs need an inhaler. The environment, our environment, continues to be diminished. So it feels slightly miraculous to have planted trees, allowing them to form the boundaries, to add definition, as well as providing habitat, colour and, one day, fruit. In the doing of this, as my friends and I stamped about in clay-mud, cold-fingered, longing for hot cups of tea, it would seem that a dream was fulfilled, that I am the steward of a little orchard. In one way, I am. There are more than five fruit trees. But in another way, I'm not. I'm the owner, the custodian, of some fruit trees, not an orchard. The serried ranks of fruit trees in a meadow, perhaps with geese keeping guard, beehives in the background, still beckons as a distinct dream. I've arrived, but not arrived, simultaneously. Perhaps I'm simply on a road that, until now, I didn't know existed and the journey is the thing, not the arrival.

The Highcliffe Allotments, where my little plot (103b) is to be found, are a hidden world behind a locked gate to keep out vandals. They are a higgledy-piggledyness of sheds, green-houses and polytunnels. There are also, charmingly, goats, sheep, pigs, chickens and bees. Though the M3 roars past, less than a mile away, they are nonetheless a place of tranquillity and solace. Here, there are no emails. The phone doesn't ring. And there are no deadlines. On the first day of the year, that sense of tranquillity is profound. At 10.30 a.m., I am the only person here. Presumably, everyone else is nursing a hangover from last night's celebrations.

My little plot, this blessed plot, is in reality roughly 40 feet squared of unloved clay, which when I first saw it was buried somewhere beneath knee-high grass and waist-high rubbish. It lies towards the end of the south-facing site, along a rutted track. The allotments are tucked in between a housing estate and sports fields, on the side of a hill. It's hardly glamorous. I'm towards the bottom of the slope, but still just about have a view over the boundary hedge to where football and cricket are played. Girls' football teams play on a Saturday morning, and the sound of cheering parents, appealing children and the ref's whistle forms a regular backdrop to my digging.

There are other sounds too: the bleating of the goats, the baaing of lambs and sheep, cockerels crowing, bees buzz-ing, honking geese and birds singing. It's easy not to hear the motorway.

I'm surrounded by other plots, all done in different styles. On one side are the allotment manager Jim and his wife Rose. Their plot is immaculate. Flowers and vegetables stand neatly in rows. No weed would dare to attempt to grow there. They are retired and are always happy to stop, chat and offer advice and encouragement.

Alongside them are Fran and Ian, a busy working couple, who arrive in a selection of swanky cars, work hard and stay late into the evening. Between my plot and the allotment bound-ary is an extensive plot belonging to Merv and Val. They've had their plot for years and run it like a well-oiled machine in spring and summer: polytunnels, greenhouses and the soil itself all producing considerable crops for them. Well-established apple, damson and plum trees border their plot. To my right are a couple of archaeologists, whom I seldom see. Their plot is set up with raised beds and is neat and ordered, if not often visited. The plot above me has also received a new tenant in the last year: Dan, a young Canadian chef, who works in a characterful local pub.

Dan's plot and mine were formerly one and hadn't been tended for a long time. After much clearing, I discovered a garden table, chairs and parasol that were initially invisible to the naked eye because of all of the junk and undergrowth covering them. It was that bad. Dan has cut his back and has really enjoyed growing food as well as cooking it. Slowly, over many months, with the help of friends, I'd chipped away at my plot, drawing and re-drawing the general layout of the thing on scraps of paper. In six months, it had changed from a site of desolation with two collapsing sheds to a nearly-completely-fenced site with seven fruit trees, raspberry canes, a restored shed painted blue and green and a second-hand octagonal greenhouse. To enrich the soil, I had ferried sack after sack, barrowload after barrowload of manure down to the various beds that were now marked out. Now, on the cusp of my first full year on the plot, there was one corner left to dig before the ice came, and today was the day to do it.

Under a peerless blue sky, I start to dig the last corner of what will become the herbaceous border. The border is extensive, but the last patch is a 6 foot by 4 foot area that currently only sports dandelions, mallow and speedwell. But this year alliums, salvias and roses will take their place.

Digging is immensely satisfying. Unlike an awful lot of life, when you dig, you see results quickly. After 45 minutes, I have a neatly dug, weed-free patch of earth, with a reassuring number of earthworms. Digging is also meditative. The stresses of the day invariably drift away as I dig. The internal clutter in my head is swept out. Ideas come unbidden into my mind. With a calmer frame of mind, it's also then possible to start to take in what's going on around me. I am a visitor here. But the allotments are a permanent home to wildlife, and the quietness of my mind allows me to pay attention to it.

Over the pealing of bells – a sound which is quintessentially

Winchester to me – comes another that also speaks of home: the 'chack, chack' of the jackdaw. There are several nests in my road, nearby, and the sound of the jackdaws chattering away to one another is often the first thing I hear in the morning. It conjures up comfort and family, even if that family is feathered, not human. For 25 years they have lived there and are just as much my neighbours as any of the people in the street. So, when I hear a raucous 'chack-chacking', I lean on my spade and look up, as between 40 and 50 jackdaws wheel overhead, settling in the two giant beech trees at the top of the allotments.

As at home, I'm trying to welcome in the birds, so that they will become my partners in keeping down the numbers of aphids, slugs and snails in the summer. After an adult lifetime of doing this, I have robins, blackbirds, blackcaps, wrens, collared doves and a hedge full of sparrows nesting at home. They are joined every morning by a noisy, boisterous bunch of starlings, who feed on the leftover hen food and lard I mix for them. But the day I saw my first thrush in the garden was a cause for celebration. It has nested there for the last two years, killing all the snails, smashing them to bits on the patio.

I'd like to welcome in the allotment birds, and so have hung a bird feeder on the Victoria plum tree that is my plot inheritance and my pride and joy. Feathers suggest that only a pigeon and a magpie have eaten from it. But as the surrounding hedgerows are alive with sparrows, I hope that they, at least, are helping themselves.

When I get home, almost psychotically tired, a red kite is wheeling slowly over the street. It feels like a good omen for the year ahead. Red kites are majestic birds, and that has been part of their problem. Egg collectors robbed at least a quarter of their nests. Birds were poisoned and killed. In the 1950s and 60s, attempts were made to protect existing nests, and my father, a keen ornithologist, was part of that endeavour. Yet red kites remained among the three most threatened bird species in the UK, so, in the 1980s, a reintroduction scheme was hatched. At first, they were a rare sight. Then they started to expand their territory. Over years of commuting along the M4,

I watched them travel east, then slowly south along the A34. But this is the first time I've seen a red kite over Winchester. My father, now long dead, would have been overjoyed. I'm too tired to dance, but inwardly, I'm celebrating. The past and future have coalesced in that soaring bird. Like the kite, I am spreading my wings to fly into my future.

Energy has not returned, when, two days later, I head back to the allotment, for the biggest piece of preparation yet: arranging paths. Once I'd hacked down to the ground through the jungle and wreckage that I found, there were two small vegetable beds and lots of grass. I've drawn and re-drawn the plan.

The end result is: two fruit beds, two vegetable beds, a herbaceous border, seating area, greenhouse, shed and water butts. To connect all these, I need paths. These are to be of woodchip, so that no mowing is involved.

I spend a freezing afternoon under a bitter winter's sky laying black weed suppressing membrane, which will form the basis of the paths, and then laying wooden planks around it to form the edges. It looks like nothing but an exercise in faith, 'the substance of things hoped for, but not seen'. Much of that time I am swearing at a nameless, invasive weed, which I thought I'd completely eradicated through much digging, but have not. It's growing back underneath the weed-suppressing membrane. The cheek of it. To vent my fury, I've dubbed it the Boris Johnson weed. 'I hate you. I really hate you,' I say to it, on my knees, muddy, cognizant that I will lose this battle. Repeatedly. Whether I'm talking to the weed or the politician is up for debate.

The job of actually creating the paths is beyond me. My allotment neighbours James and Nikki have volunteered to help. They are fiercely practical. I am not. Nikki saws the wood. James directs. I am charged with lots of hammering. The inevitable happens as I miss a nail and hit my left index finger, which instantly becomes a purple-and-black P-shape. It hurts mightily, and the air is bitterly cold. But we persist, and at the end of a gruelling day the plot has taken shape, its two long vegetable borders and two fruit beds clearly defined by the wood. Even the quirkily shaped herbaceous border now has structure. My hopes might be about to be realized.

A local tree surgeon, Mark Merritt, has agreed to meet me at the allotments at 9 a.m. the following day to deliver wood-chip to create the paths, so I arrive ten minutes early. It is profoundly, deep-mid-winterly cold. The earth is hard as iron. The sky is light grey. Everything else is white with a thick frost. Two pigeons sit hunched against the cold in a nearby tree.

I pace up and down waiting for Mark and see who really lives here. Blackbirds, robins, starlings, sparrows, dunnocks, long-tailed tits and, joy of joys, several thrushes. A skein of geese flies overhead, honking. A sandy-coloured cat, large-eyed and fluffed up against the cold, comes out hunting. There are undoubtedly rats. He has a job to do. He trots past on a mission.

Smoke rises from a chimney in one of the sheds. I'm not alone after all. There is another car. But it is frosted over. Whoever lit the fire might have been here all night. I am clad head-to-toe in thermals, but after ten minutes of pacing, I am chilled to the bone. So I knock on the shed's door and ask admittance into the warmth.

Nick is a former member of the armed forces. He's seen action and done ceremonial duty for the Queen. He was shot while on a tour of duty in Northern Ireland. But it was less than a year ago that he was diagnosed with PTSD.

Two days after Christmas, his relationship ended. He packed a bag and has been sleeping in the shed ever since. His military background means that he can make something out of nothing. He has the fire going; a two-hob cooker and a sink. But it's a shed. And he has served his country. He offers me a cup of tea and a place by the fire and tells his tale.

As a foreign reporter, I've spent much of my career in people's homes listening to their stories. It's taught me that we are essentially the same. Sitting in the kitchen of a refugee shelter in the Middle East is not so different from being in a mud hut in Burkina Faso or a chateau in France, or, as now, Nick's shed.

I sit and listen. An hour passes in a breath. I am warm again. And, without doubt, the most important bit of the day has already happened. It was not making the paths, it was stopping and listening, while receiving a warm welcome from a person who needed help.

Mark and his cockapoo, Berkeley, arrive, with a lorryload of chippings from fir and holly trees. Mark's the kind of tree surgeon who wants to keep trees going and flourishing, not cut them down. On the sly, his life's work is educating his customers not only to keep trees, but to plant more.

I show him the plum tree. 'It's not much of a tree, is it?' he says. On the contrary, I say, it's fantastic. You should see how much fruit it gives. Would you prune it, or is it too small a job? He circles the tree, scratching his chin. 'Well,' he says, 'we need to thin it out a bit. It's slightly congested. And these straggly bits,' he says, pointing, 'need to come off. Then it will be a nice tree, yes, a very nice tree indeed.' We agree that he'll come back when the tree is in full leaf and ready for its haircut.

I spend the rest of the day shovelling woodchip into the wheelbarrow and carting it off to the plot, and slowly creating paths. It is so slow that I have to break it down into small chunks: ten more shovelfuls and the barrow will be full; four more barrowloads and I'll be at this corner of the path; another hour and I can stop for lunch, and on it goes.

It's warming work, so despite the cold I peel off layers of clothing and hang them on a fence post. Anything is worthy of a break: watching the starlings who are mobbing the bird feeder; spotting the sheep-that-always-escapes-from-the-nearby-field head down the track; demolishing a bacon sandwich that Nick has provided.

At lunchtime, he heads for the day centre for homeless people in his 4x4, homelessness having many guises. 'They say they'll keep me a meal,' he says. When I leave as dusk is settling in, he hasn't returned, so I am hopeful that he has been given more help than just a meal. I leave a bag of fuel on his shed doorstep and am reminded of what is important in life: being, not doing.

A few days later, Rachel, a friend who's a professional gardener, comes and helps me finish the paths. It is such a radically different experience with help. She shovels woodchip,

I lay it along the paths. The whole thing is completed in the batting of an eye. I go back the next day with a sense of disbelief, just to check that it's real. It is.

Winter is traditionally hedging and ditching season. I have neither, but am planning on finishing the chestnut paling fencing that will surround the plot. It will give plants the chance to grow vertically, not just along the ground. This side-of-the-hill site is boisterously windy even on a still summer's day. Hopefully, squashes, cucumbers, peas and roses will not blow over on this fence.

You learn by your mistakes and one of mine was basic. I took the measurement of the plot on paper and ordered that amount of fencing, not factoring in that the undulating ground would make the fence not stretch so far. So, with a crew of friends to help, we got three-quarters of the way round and ran out of paling. I don't think they were surprised. I was.

Winter is the time to plan. I've drawn out a plan on paper, but, mindful of my fencing experience, I take the plan and a measuring tape to the allotment, sit and contemplate it. A lone starling comes in to see if it's possible to eat the mealworms I've put out for him while I'm there, finds that he hasn't quite got the nerve and flies off. So, unaccompanied by birds, I sit and gaze at the plot, trying to imagine its summer fullness.

Is my plan the right one? There is, of course, no such thing as a right plan. You just need the confidence to step out into whatever might come next, a mirror of the rest of life. But once everything is laid out here, there will be no going back. Now that I've given over so much space to soft fruit (wine berries, jostaberries, strawberries, redcurrants, raspberries and the fruit trees) and an extensive herbaceous border to keep me in bunches of flowers, there isn't that much room for vegetables. I measure it out and realize that it will be enough.

I've dug over two areas for vegetables, one 18 by 6 feet and the other 25 by 8 feet, and left them to the frosts and worms. However, the soil still looks grey and unpromising. Surrounding plots have friable, black soil after years of good management and nurture. No one, it would appear, has cared for this soil for a considerable time. It looks half-starved. Feed me, it says.

The standard option in these parts for feeding poor soil is to add well-rotted horse manure. And you'd be forgiven for thinking that – as a horse rider – I could lay my hands on a lot of well-rotted manure very easily. You'd be wrong. I could ask for some at the yard where I ride someone else's horse. But I know from experience that getting it involves long walks up and down steep hills with a full wheelbarrow. It's such hard work that I can't face it.

When I was looking for manure before Christmas, a friend said that they knew someone in a local village who could deliver manure at £3 per bag. I rang him to enquire. 'Winchester's too far,' he said, of a 15-minute journey. I sighed and rang the number on an advert for manure on the allotment gate. 'Yes, we can deliver,' the man said. 'That'll be £265.' For manure? 'Yes.' I don't think so. As I stamped back to my plot, incandescent at both the slothful and the extortionate muck merchants, I bumped into Pete, a semi-retired professional gardener, and one of the elders of the plots. I told him my tale of woe, simply to get it off my chest. 'I know someone with horses,' he said. 'I'll bring you some.' And he did. A week later, there was a big pile of manure near my plot.

But I've used up all of Pete's horse manure and don't want to try his patience by asking for more. So I consider my options. I've been told that fresh alpaca poo can be put straight on to vegetable plots and doesn't need to rot down first, unlike horse manure. If this is the case, I'm in luck, as – this being Hampshire – I have a friend with a field full of alpacas. It turns out to be true. 'Sprinkle it lightly across the vegetable plots and water it in,' is the advice from someone who uses the stuff regularly. Alpaca poo: the solution for the poor, grey soil, and possibly the craziest thing I've considered thus far. I have crossed a Rubicon.

The voice of the undernourished vegetable plot reached further than my ears. It lifted on the wind and was caught by people with plenty of well-rotted manure to spare. I know this because I don't ask for muck, it comes to me. The friend with the alpacas offers to collect their poo, which is something akin to large rabbit droppings, for a week. That will give me several sackfuls, which can go on the ground straightaway. While she's busy scraping up alpaca poo for me, I receive a call from an old horse-riding acquaintance. She's sorting out the muck heap at her yard. There is stuff that's several years old, black gold, more than ready to go on to the sorry ground and lift the spirits of the worms. Would I like it? Of course I would.

I drive round early the next morning when the world is half-asleep and everything is layered in a thick, white frost. Every twig is covered. Every puddle turned to ice. She has filled six capacious horse-feed bags with beautiful, well-rotted horse manure for me. These are so large that only three will fit in the car. I drive straight to the allotment and pour out the frozen contents on to the soil. You can almost hear the soil sigh with relief. Then I head back across town for the rest.

Most of the vegetable beds now have nourishment, but there is still room for the alpaca poo. What I can safely tell you is that it is impossible to sprinkle it on to the soil. The two-pound-coin-sized droppings clump together and refuse to shake loose. I imagined myself sprinkling alpaca poo on to the soil like sugar on to cereal. Instead, I'm laying clods of the stuff here and there and, even with a strong fork, can't break them up. I sigh. This is a job for the experts: I leave it to the worms. They have three months to pull everything down into the soil before planting is set to begin.

I have the industrial revolution to thank for my plot, if inadvertently. Allotment holding dates back hundreds of years, but the system that we recognize today, and that I'm now part of, has its roots in the nineteenth century. Land was given over to the working poor, who were in desperate need of it, due to rapid industrialization and the growth of towns.

In 1908 the Smallholdings and Allotments Act came into force, obliging local authorities to set land aside for people to grow their own food. It wasn't until the 1920s that this really took hold in a big way. In 1929 the Winchester New Allotment Holders Society was formed, providing plots in one area of the city. Today there are 12 sites across and around the city, with more than 400 members. It is cheering to discover that our site is, in fact, the oldest of them all. No law was needed to kick-start our south-facing, twelve-and-a-half acre site. It began in 1907 and today has around 100 members. The land was ultimately bought from the Church Commissioners and is owned and run by the allotments' members.

What marks our site out is the livestock. Growing your own vegetables is now fashionable, desirable, and people are queuing for plots. As I write looking back on this year of growing, during the coronavirus pandemic, the desire to be outside away from people has led to a surge in demand. There's a 27-strong waiting list on our site. This wasn't always the case. So, during a lull in proceedings when plots couldn't be filled, they were joined up to form small fields on which it's possible to keep livestock, once you've been an allotment holder for a year and proved, one supposes, that you can be trusted, and turn up even if it snows.

This January, there are several small flocks of sheep, bee-hives, two large cream-coloured goats that eat everything, including Christmas trees, and innumerable chickens. There were a couple of pigs (Pinky and Perky) who, I think, may have become sausages. I walk along the path that takes me to the fields, thinking covetous, impractical thoughts. I would love a field. But I have no husbandry skills, except for taking care of hens. What would I keep? How would I manage? Could I have a plot where a proper orchard could be grown, geese kept, even bees? I lodge it in the back of my mind as a realizable dream in the future, the real fulfilment of the tree-planting passion. Dreams really can come true, it seems. So, one day, potentially, I could keep my own livestock as well as fruit and vegetables, have an orchard that actually looks like one worthy of the name. Right now, however, back in the real world, I must address myself to a plan for vegetables. It's time to prepare for the next stage of this unexpected adventure.

FEBRUARY

Structure

I've spent more than 30 years as a journalist, and though I'm now set on a slightly different course as a project manager, I'm still a journalist to my core. In journalism you learn early on that structure is key: the structure of the day, knowing the best time to pitch a story and when to file it; but also, crucially, the structure of your story. You can have the best story in the world, but if you can't string it together sensibly, if its structure is poor, it won't be read. Writing well is about asking yourself what you want to say, to whom. It's working out what you've got to say, and then saying it, and then ensuring that people know you've said it.

Within this structure, there is a thing of beauty: the nut graf. In features, this is where you outline the essence of your story. Designing an allotment, it turns out, requires much the same approach. The allotment must have a coherent physical structure; it must be possible to divide the plants into their different groupings; and to do that you have to know what you're doing and why. It's storytelling with vegetables instead of words.

So what's my allotment nut graf? What am I trying to do? If I know that, it will lead inexorably to the structure of the plot. Initially, as well as planting a small orchard, it was to keep myself in salad crops and never to buy a cucumber wrapped in plastic ever again. That a cucumber should be wrapped in plastic shows you that quite a bit has gone wrong with the world. Back in 2016, a member of the House of Lords appealed for cucumbers not to be wrapped in plastic anymore. The wonderfully named Cucumber Growers' Association estimated that some 470 tonnes of plastic waste from UK-bought cucumbers would be saved. Annually.

The good news is that cucumbers are no longer wrapped in plastic during the summer, when they can be bought from the UK. But here's the thing: if you buy a cucumber in November, it won't be grown in the UK. So it will have travelled. And will be wrapped in plastic. Why buy a cucumber in November? It makes no sense, and it's having a negative effect on the planet. Think of the food miles. And the plastic. I'm not about to take on the Big Four supermarkets, but by growing and eating in season, a little change can be wrought even on a little plot like this or, indeed, in a back garden. I'd like to be self-sufficient in vegetables from June to Christmas, and to have enough to give away. But I also want to take fruit and flowers home. These wishes determine not only the structure of the plot, but its content, and they will determine the structure of many hours of my time over the coming year. After all, you have to set a goal before you can travel towards it.

Despite all this, February is the month for twiddling your thumbs. It's not all action. It's as if the earth is holding its breath, waiting for spring and the burgeoning activity it will bring. 'Not yet,' says the soil. 'Not yet,' says the thermometer. 'Not yet,' says everything within me, though a small voice is asking, 'When then?' This is an object lesson in stopping and resting, as well as being busy. The earth needs a rest, and arguably so do I.

However, I've joined a couple of allotment groups online and find that, around the country, people are itching to get growing. The days are stretching out. My three back-garden hens (Bandit, Ivy and Honeysuckle) are now refusing to go to bed until 5.15 p.m., whereas in December, by 4.30 p.m. they were on their perches. With the lengthening days comes a primal feeling that the growing season is upon us. It is, if you have a heated greenhouse and know what you're doing. It isn't, if like me, you have an unheated greenhouse and don't.

Seed packets say, 'plant indoors between January and March', which makes February definitely an option. But golden days in February are a false spring. Snow can fall any time between now and Easter, which this year is at the back end of April. Frosts are a likelihood too. So any small seed started off too early can perish in later cold weather. I am mindful that this time last year, parts of the UK were under 12 inches of snow. I'm also aware that climate change means that our already unpredictable spring weather is now even more unpredictable, and unpredictability is bad for seedlings.

Nonetheless, I am rueing the day that I failed to pay more attention to my father. Having a large plot of land, we were self-sufficient in vegetables, and in fruit during the summer and autumn. I helped out as a child, but my knowledge is much more about weeding, harvesting and, frankly, eating than it is about when to start growing things.

The greenhouse was my father's territory. Unless you were Paddy, the cat, you had to ask permission to enter. Paddy (a big, tabby-and-white farm cat) spent a lot of time asleep on a pile of hessian sacks in the greenhouse, as my father tended his seedlings. Nonetheless, he doubtless picked up some knowledge about planting times and how to care for seeds. I didn't.

So it is that I find myself experiencing a loss of nerve. In the first few months of having the plot, I planted a few things in the small bits of unpromising ground that were available. The sun shone. I watered every day. As a consequence, I kept myself in salad stuff from June to November, had plenty of squashes over winter and am still harvesting a line of perpetual spinach that lived up to its name.

But now, on the cusp of my first full growing season, with the long winter to think about it, I've got the allotment holder's equivalent of stage fright. Can I do this? Will I make dreadful mistakes? Will anything grow? So I plan, and tell myself that not too much can go wrong. Plants want to grow. Despite my inexperience, there will be enough to eat.

It is one of life's pleasures to sit down with an array of seed packets. It's like looking at hope, the future and many uncooked meals simultaneously. What a tingle of joy it gives me. The plan – or nut graf – is quite simple: to keep myself in salad vegetables (lettuces, leaves, tomatoes and cucumbers) over the summer; and to grow as many green vegetables as possible throughout the year. Squashes, of which I'm a particular fan, will be grown along the not-quite-completed fence. Squashes take up an inordinate amount of space, which I don't have. But they are vines, and so can grow up the fence, sparing precious ground space for other things. It's not complicated.

Common sense dictates that I should only grow what I enjoy eating. That sounds sensible, doesn't it? But already, I've come across lots of people who are planting things for novelty value, or because they can be planted at this given moment, who aren't considering whether or not they like eating them. This has me scratching my head. It seems like the gardening equivalent of buying three-for-two deals in supermarkets. You might not want them, but something lures you in. I'm not being seduced by things I don't like, need or want on the plot. Let's hope that spills out into the rest of life, where it isn't, currently, true, and regrettable shopping often happens.

As well as multitudinous salad crops, I have seeds for Swiss chard, purple sprouting broccoli, pak choi, turnips, beetroot, French beans, peas, curly kale, Romanesco and, the comedy purchase, chickpeas.

Chickpeas! The packet was in the 50p sale, and I was grabbed by the total unknown quality of planting them. I don't even know what a chickpea plant looks like, let alone how to grow it. But it would be fun to try and find out, and, if the sun shines and I can harvest enough to make my own hummus, I will be ridiculously happy, and possibly smug.

The dining room table is covered in seed packets. I draw up a comprehensive list on lined paper, with columns for when the seed should be sown, then planted out and finally harvested, as well as timings for a second planting. The structure of my year is forming right there. The ability to buy anything at any time, in any season, has taken us away from the growing seasons, the sense of how long something takes from sowing to harvest, and all the stages in between. The act of planning refocuses my inner eyes from the shops' shelves to the earth and my place in it. It is a reminder of the need to nurture the soil, the seeds, the seedlings, ultimately the plants, and that the quality of the care I give will result in the harvest nurturing me. There's a broader lesson in that.

A second sowing is on my list, as I failed to do that in the last year and it was a rookie error. I had a row of seven cut-and-come-again lettuces. You're meant to take leaves every day, the plant regrows and you come back for more. I ate salad twice a day throughout the summer and couldn't keep up. Seven plants were too many. In the end, they bolted and had to be given to the hens, for whom this was birthday and Christmas simultaneously. Then there was nothing. No lettuce. And there was a considerable pause while a few new plants grew. Lesson learned, I will plant fewer this year, with a second planting later on to see me through the summer. That's the theory anyway. By the end of the year I'll know whether or not it works.

The vegetable list runs over a page-and-a-half of A4 paper. Then I take out a third sheet and reorganize it into months, with columns for when things should be sown indoors, outdoors and planted out. This is both helpful and the cause of the rabbit-in-the-headlights terror. The list says that by now I should have sown seeds indoors for beef tomatoes, Ailsa Craig tomatoes (little red ones) and even smaller yellow tomatoes. Coriander should have gone outside. This month, I should be sowing both winter mix salad and radishes.

Why does this freeze me into inactivity? First, because I've only just sprinkled alpaca poo everywhere and my helpers, the worms, tell me they need a good couple of months to assimilate it into the soil. Then there's the fact that the greenhouse isn't heated. I can't sow in there, even though it is south facing. So I ask my 91-year-old mother for advice. There would be, she says, nothing lost by planting a few tomato seeds now and putting them on the windowsill in the kitchen. If they don't do well, or do too well, needing to be planted out before the weather is clement, then I can always plant more. My father did this. I can dimly recall little rows of plant pots, covered over with small clear plastic bags or broken pieces of glass to create warmth, on our kitchen window when I was a child.

I seek a follow-up opinion, idiotically, from the social media fora and get as many answers as there are people. But the gist of it is that there's never any harm in waiting. And wait we must, because a gardener must wait until the soil is warm enough to plant in. How do you know it's warm enough? Traditionally, take your pants down and if it doesn't feel cold to your uncovered bottom, it'll be fine for seeds and plants.

It snows. I am wearing thermals. I won't be trying this method of soil testing any time soon. Instead, I walk gingerly over the hill to the allotment to feed the birds. This time I see not just thrushes, but their near-relatives, redwings, with the distinctive red patch under their wing. They live in Britain between September and April and are generally to be spotted in woodland. But, on a cold day, like thrushes, they will come out into society, looking for berries and any scraps that may be found.

There are berries aplenty along the allotment's hedges. Around the gate, ivy abounds, and its black berries are popular with birds in this cold weather. The ivy is also home to a roost of sparrows – as endless twittering attests – but it is a big draw for the redwings, who, in the heavily falling snow, are arranged along the hedge eating as many berries as they can, before an early dusk falls.

Again, I am alone. I trudge through the unblemished snow and fill the feeder with mealworms. I hope it will keep a few birds going overnight. We're in this together. If I take care of them now, they'll help me by eating unwanted insects and slugs.

No smoke rises from Nick's chimney. The local council has found him emergency accommodation. He is warm, safe and, crucially, in the system for getting better accommodation, benefits and the support that he needs.

After the snow, gales. Storm Eric blows through the south of England, bringing destruction and heavy rain. I wait some more. I tell myself there will be plenty of days in the summer when such idleness would be attractive, when I will be at the allotment after work, before work, in every nook and cranny of the time available to me, just to keep up, so I should enjoy it now, not wish it away. The truth is, I find it hard to stop. Perhaps I'm not alone. But it's easy to confuse meaning and purpose with busyness. Waiting and resting are important lessons to learn, and ones that the soil and the seasons can teach us.

In the rule of thirds, no more than a third of one's allotment can be given over to physical structures such as greenhouses, sheds and polytunnels, or indeed to trees. Everything in moderation is the message: advice for life. The allotments are a shambles of structures: sheds with full cooking facilities, woodburning stoves and sofas, others full of stored vegetables and neatly aligned tools, polytunnels that smell of summer and summerhouses that protect you from the weather in winter.

Stories of greenhouses and polytunnels becoming airborne in gales are legendary. Strong winds can lift an ill-secured greenhouse or polytunnel and relocate it, against its owners' wishes. I've seen it happen. My greenhouse is second-hand. A neighbour moved out of our road into what can only be described as a serious, grown-up house a few miles away. With the house came a small eight-sided greenhouse. She was never going to use it, she said. Would I like it?

I was thrilled. My friend, former boss and neighbour, Geordie, helped me move it and I can safely say that it was one of the most stressful things I've ever done, all the time knowing that you could break glass. And we did. Six panes went in an entirely preventable accident that was wholly my fault. As we removed panes of glass, carefully, from the greenhouse, I'd leaned them up against the nearby garden furniture, instead of the house wall, further away. The predictable catastrophe happened as we were nearly finished, the whole lot crashing over in slow motion, Geordie and I frozen to the spot. I'm still kicking myself about it now. But, on a positive note, had I bought that greenhouse new it would have cost me £850. I spent less than £100 on new glass and the very solid base it's built on: a bargain. And the greenhouse itself is perfectly serviceable. Had I not wanted it, it might have gone into landfill. The idea is unthinkable.

My allotment neighbours, Nikki and James, advised on keeping the greenhouse stable (and not airborne). So we had spent another day fixing the greenhouse to a wooden base. Then there were a couple more days spent putting the glass back in. As we put the final pane in, we heard the tinkling of a thousand tiny bells behind us. Turning slowly, as if in a dream, we saw that a nearby greenhouse, also recently erected and glazed but not secured to a solid base, had taken off in the wind and flown about 20 feet across the allotments. The next hour was spent moving it back and picking up tiny fragments of glass.

Storm Eric saw winds gust up to 70 mph; so, fearing the worst and hoping for the best, I trudge round to the allotment to see what damage has been caused. It's good news. The greenhouse and shed are intact. Only one sheet of black, weed-suppressing membrane has been wrenched out of the ground. That's all. I'm relieved. As I turn to go, I spot something that wasn't there before: my fence is complete. The Allotment Faeries have been out finishing it for me, in the manner of the cobbler's assistants in the fairy tale.

I stand and cry. This speaks of an incredible generosity of spirit, kindness and thoughtfulness, that sees people finish off a job for someone else and not mention that they did it. This is community in action. It's not what I've been used to in the sharp-elbowed world of work, but increasingly find is normal behaviour in the parallel universe of the allotments. The milk of human kindness still runs freely here.

The Allotment Faeries are easy to detect, despite their modesty: Nikki and James. They joined the allotments just a few months ago, but being practical people, their plot already looks as if they've had it for years. They are the people who I ask when I don't know what I'm doing, which is quite a bit of the time. And they are people I would simply never have met if our plots weren't 50 yards apart. James works nights at a leading supermarket. They live in a nearby village. They are bikers. James sports long grey hair, an equally lengthy beard and has many piercings. They are among the kindest, warmest-hearted people you could ever hope to meet. Our shared love of gardening and the great outdoors far outweighs any outward differences. I ring to thank them. 'Don't be daft,' says Nikki.

With that one act of kindness, the plot is complete. A winter of creating a layout, making paths, planting trees, moving raspberry canes, erecting a greenhouse and putting up a fence, is over. The little plot is as ready as it's going to be to start producing vegetables, fruit and flowers.

The flowers were an afterthought. Actually, they weren't my idea at all. I was all for serried ranks of vegetables. My mother pitched for a small area of flowers. 'You'll be able to take bunches of flowers home,' she said. As I love to have the house full of flowers, preferably native, scented ones, this was the best way to influence me.

Flowers aren't just pretty, they are good for you. *Psychology Today* reports that 'flowers make you happy by triggering your happy brain chemicals': dopamine, oxytocin and serotonin. So a flower bed will cheer me up, as well as brighten the home.

What began as a concessional corner to my mother has become a large irregular triangular bed around the Victoria plum tree. The idea is not just to keep my mother and me in flowers, but to provide a source of sustenance for pollinators too.

While I'm contemplating the happy readiness of the plot, a truly shocking report is published in the journal *Biological*

Conservation. It claims that the world's insects – including its pollinators – are heading towards extinction, threatening eco-systems and, essentially, life as we know it. The very life of our planet is under threat from our own behaviour.

More than 40 per cent of insect species are declining and a third are endangered, the report says. The rate of extinction is eight times faster than that of animals, birds and reptiles. But it will affect all of them too, including mankind.

Who, or what, is to blame? Intensive farming, the report claims, specifically insecticides that have been introduced in recent years containing neonicotinoids and fipronil. These, the report says, stay in the ground 'sterilizing' it and 'killing all the grubs'. Reading the report makes me feel overwhelmed and powerless. I can't save the world from itself, or more specific-ally, the folly and greed of mankind. But I can, I reason, make an environment that will attract pollinators and insects, and therefore become a habitat for all. I can make a difference in this small 40 by 40 foot plot. And if I can do it there, then others can do it in their small plots, and so I hope positive change can happen incrementally. We can all make different choices, we just need to do it. We can fight back against the chemical-spreading machine.

That's why the allotment's structure (design is too grand a word) gives such a concession to flowers. This is viewed somewhat dimly by the more traditional allotment holders, for whom vegetables are all. Undeterred, into the herbaceous border I aim to plant alliums, climbing roses to ramble along the fence, asters and peonies, with huge, plate-like flowers. They are blousy for a week and then over. But what a week it will be.

The priority is to plant flowers that will really attract pollin-ators, single blooms into which they can get easily, rather than double flowers, which present an obstacle course. And I want a decent growing season, so that I can provide nectar for the pollinators and flowers for myself from May to October. This may not be possible in my first year, but it's an ambition. So I buy seeds of California Poppy and sweet pea, which should flower from May onwards, providing early food; Toy Shop and Autumn Beauty sunflowers, which will add colour from June to September, as well as seeds for the birds in winter; and finally, tithonia Red Torch and rudbeckia Chocolate, which should be doing their thing from August to November.

Fran, a friend who is head gardener at a nearby arboretum, and therefore a good source of wisdom, suggests I buy a propagator to get my seedlings started at home. This means I don't have to worry about whether the greenhouse is too hot or cold. Diurnal temperatures (the difference between night and day) are currently extreme, with three days reaching 20 degrees, but night-time temperatures dipping below freezing. A propagator will remain at a constant 16 degrees, giving my little seeds the chance to emerge into a well-regulated, comfortable world.

So, one sunny Sunday afternoon at the end of the month, I take myself outside with serried ranks of seeds, small pots and a bucket of compost to start the process. Beef tomatoes, small red tomatoes and little yellow tomatoes are all planted. Then it's time for the flowers: sweet peas, achillea (a yellow, plate-shaped flower) and tithonia Red Torch, orange daisy-like flowers borne on a mass of 5-foot stems.

These are the first to emerge after a few days. In one day, the earliest seedlings grow a full inch. I can now understand why planting too early is a bad idea. You could almost watch them grow. The tomatoes are slower to get going. But by the end of the first week I have one tiny green seedling emerging from the soil. I smile. They are prolific. By July or August, I'll be taking home bags of little yellow tomatoes from this single plant.

Back at the allotments, I sit in the early spring sunshine chatting to the allotment manager. He has a small, south-facing bench on his plot, which even at this time of year is a delightfully sheltered and warm place to sit. He has heard a rumour, he says, that Dan, who works the plot adjacent to mine, may be leaving the country later this year. Would I like his plot too if this happens?

He knows I would. I've already put my name down for it in the spirit of empire-building, in the hope that one day, years hence, it will become free. I wasn't expecting that any time soon; after all, like me, Dan's not been working the plot for long. Half a plot is great, but just think what I could grow with a full plot. How did I get to this point where, already, I want more? Part of me is thrilled. I imagine myself buying cherry trees, erecting a polytunnel and building an archway for squashes. Part of me is maddeningly frustrated. I've just finished the fencing and tree-planting. Had I known this earlier, I'd have created a very different plot. The structure would have been entirely different. Now the trees are planted, there's no going back. I swallow down the annoyance and do a little jig. 'Don't celebrate too soon,' he says. 'It's not yours yet.' He promises to ring Dan and find out if he really will be giving up the plot, because now is a good moment to let someone else (me) at it, if he is, though if Dan's leaving the country later in the year, this might be a bit previous, as surely he'll want to keep growing until he leaves?

I spend a week running ideas through my head of what I'd do with the space, which is currently a wasteland. A chef's life is a busy one and after a summer of growing, Dan's been tied to the kitchen over the winter, and nature has fought back on his side of the fence. A polytunnel would be an important purchase, extending the growing season and allowing me to grow things that won't flourish either outside or in the small, eight-sided greenhouse. Among those things that I'm now seriously considering are a dessert grapevine and sweet potato plants. How did that happen?

I research self-fertile cherry trees that grow on dwarf rooting stock and even work out what kind of cage I'll build to protect them from the starlings: wooden stakes covered with netting. This, I figure, will be adaptable and can change as the trees grow. I contemplate buying a selection of gooseberry bushes to grow in the semi-shade of my apple trees. It doesn't feel like a firm vision, but it's the beginnings of a plan. Phil, one of my best friends, puts in a request for me to grow Crown Prince squashes when I get the plot. They are, he pronounces, the tastiest squash there is, and he'd like me to supply both those and also salsify, please.

It's a good job that I decide to wait before buying the seeds. On the last day of February, I go to the allotments to measure out the areas of my existing vegetable beds that will be given over to each type of vegetable. To keep the soil healthy, it's best to rotate crops, not plant them in the same space each year. To do that, you divide all the vegetables into four different types: brassicas (cabbages, purple sprouting broccoli, kale); tomatoes (including cucumbers); onions (including leeks and garlic) and beans. Then I need to squeeze in a few more things: squash, corn, leafy greens and lettuce. I'm like a set designer apportioning space to the different elements of their stage set.

As I arrive, I can see that my dreams of expansion won't be realized just yet. Having not been around all winter, having left leeks and beetroot in the ground for months, there is evidence that Dan is obviously still in the country and keen to get growing again. Like Mole in *Wind in the Willows*, he's emerged with the spring. A quarter of his plot has already been dug over and covered with the ubiquitous black weed-suppressing membrane. A second quarter is partially dug.

Damn it. Thou shalt not covet thy neighbour's ass, as the Bible has it, or, it would seem, their allotment either. As I'm about to leave, he arrives, smiling, endearing, shabby, the dog-end of a roll-up cigarette partly smoked, handsome in a not-quite-out-of-short-trousers way. 'I heard you were leaving the country,' I say. 'Oh no,' he replies. 'I want to get a visa extension, but I'll have to go back in the summer to apply.' 'What do you want to happen?' I ask. 'I want to stay,' he says.

And with that, all dreams of cherry trees, a grapevine, gooseberry bushes, sweet potatoes and extensive squash-growing evaporate. I smile, 'That's great,' I say. I like Dan. But I am middle-aged so I will play the long game. One day, surely, he will get bored or open his own restaurant and be too busy to have an allotment; and then, the empire will strike back.

One last, resolutely quirky thing happens before February concedes ground to March. A troupe of musicians and performers has decided to stage a production about the *Day of the Triffids*, retelling it, as far as I can understand, in the context of, or through the lens of, local allotment holders.

So, on a day when snow and gales have been replaced by summer temperatures, I meet the artistic director-cum-producer and sound recordist at the allotments. This is cosmic payback. As a journalist I've been asking people questions for more than 30 years. So when someone else wants to ask questions, I should put myself forward to answer them.

The producer asks why I wanted the allotment in the first place. I explain about trees, orchards, my childhood, the joy of now having seven fruit trees. 'What do you think will still be here in 20 years' time?' she asks. Well, obviously the trees. Imagine, maturing trees producing a respectable harvest.

'Tell me about the worst weed,' she says. I explain about the nameless weed and how I hate it, how I know I will lose, how it makes me want to weep, how it is inextricably linked in my mind with Boris Johnson. She gives me the thumbs up: this is exactly what she wants – hatred of the invasive species, dislike of politicians.

Then she asks the clincher. 'What scares you?' 'Oh, the whole thing,' I say blithely. 'What if I get it wrong? What if I kill plants off? It's all so unknown.' She smiles. 'And in the rest of life?' Suddenly we appear to have gone through a door into a therapy session. I talk about my fear of situations that go badly awry, in which I have no control and can make no impact. I don't explain why this is the case and mercifully she doesn't ask. I don't want to talk about my father's years of mental illness, about the daily worry if he was still alive, or dead. But I am determined that the fear will not thrive here. I'll get it under control, perhaps better than Boris Johnson weed. By the end of the year, I'll have grown my own fruit, flowers and vegetables.

I'll have failures and successes, and I'll learn from all of them. And I'll have discovered whether my structure works or not. This is growing after all, not sculpture, so if it doesn't work, it can be changed. There's freedom from fear in that. March beckons: the month for serious planting and preparedness. The gun is about to be fired in the race of my year.

MARCH

Hope

This is the month of hope. Having staggered through the winter, dodging colds and flu, scraping ice from the car, travelling to and from work in the dark, barely seeing the sky during the day, but being very familiar with the moon and streetlights, I can now smell the spring. Days are lengthening. The equinox will bring that most treasured of things, evenings, and with them a sense of freedom, of emerging, like Mole, into the light. The earth is readying itself for another season of growth, and so am I.

Audrey Hepburn once said, 'To plant a garden is to believe in tomorrow.' She was right. Sowing seeds is one of life's most hopeful activities. It sets your sights beyond today, to a point that you cannot see and may not live to experience. It speaks of an unknown future, of an unimaginable harvest, of warm days and fresh produce heading straight to the table.

According to the notes on virtually all my seed packets, now is the time to start planting, at least in pots on a warm window-sill. Few things can stand the unpredictability and downright chilliness of March, even though we are in southern England.

The exception to this is broad beans. On the first Sunday of the month, I am at the Winchester farmers' market, to do what amounts to my bimonthly shop, when, out of the corner of my eye, I spot them. The nurserymen are slowly returning to the market, having spent the winter nurturing plants and bulbs into life, leaving their pitches to the sellers of game, bread and vegetables. But a few are back already, like the blackbirds in my garden, who are getting ahead of the game by making an early nest.

I've been shopping at the farmers' market for about 20 years and remember its former glory, the days when it was the biggest market of its kind in the country, with some 96 stalls, bustling with shoppers, thick with creaky-kneed farmers in misshapen tweed coats and Aigle wellies. All the food comes from a 30-mile radius, so it is fresh, local and seasonal; surely so much better than a supermarket and its endless plastic and food miles. But things have changed. First came the financial crisis. Shoppers had less disposable income and retreated. The cost of stalls (always pricey) has risen, the number of stall holders has diminished and, in an unvirtuous circle, so the number of customers has fallen away too, until this once-glorious market is now just a shadow of its former self.

I still have friends who sell there. I wouldn't buy anywhere else. But I rather suspect that, if this lack of investment and nurture goes on, the market will perish. I'm shaken out of these dismal thoughts and into a more hopeful demeanour by the nurseryman, who has a host of wonderful things on offer, including broad beans. Elderly, white-haired, slightly stooped, suited and booted in wellies and tweed, he perches on a high stool and dispenses wisdom. The broad beans are, he says, a short-stemmed variety, better for my windy, exposed plot. They won't mind the cold. They can even stand frosts. Nine plants for £1.50. Sold.

The plants are just 3 inches tall. They need hardening off (acclimatizing to outdoor spring temperatures, by leaving them outside during the day and bringing them in at night). I do this, and contemplate what support they might need once planted out. Brushy twigs would appear to be the right kind of height, giving the plants something to grip on to and grow into. So as I drive to work or out socially, I keep half an eye open for twigs by the side of the road. I do this with the other eye open to the law. It is illegal to remove wood from someone's property without asking. So if you ever see a pile of wood that looks like it might make a very handy lot of logs for your fire, knock on the person's door and enquire about whether or not they want it. Don't just shove it in the boot of your car and head for home. The reason is simple: you're taking not just someone's property, but potentially the means of heating their home.

Does this extend to twigs? I'm a bit hazy on this point. So I eschew quite a number of potential piles of twigs just in case. Then, one Saturday in early March, I visit my friend Annie and her magnificent Shire horse, Lady, in the depths of the Hampshire countryside. Lady is stabled in a plot that includes a seventeenth-century thatched barn. The lane on which the stable stands is only frequented by farmers, residents, horse riders, cyclists, a few hardy joggers and delivery drivers. It is quiet and forgotten. On the way home, in a layby, are branches cut down from overhanging shrubs in the winter. They have nice, twiggy ends. I park, break up a boot-full and head home, supports for the broad beans now provided.

The patch of ground designated for the broad beans has been covered with well-rotted horse manure and black weed-suppressing membrane. I hope that a transformation has happened. In reality, like most of life, the results are mixed. The good news is that the soil is full of worms of every kind: long, snake-like ones, smaller ones, little red ones that I associate with compost heaps and wormeries. It's a big improvement on last year, when there was just one solitary worm.

On the surface, it may appear that I'm working this plot alone. But below the surface, I am not. The earthworms are my constant help. There are 27 varieties of earthworm in the UK and their habitats are as varied as any other creature. Some live in compost, others create burrows deep underground, and still more create a network of tunnels in the mid-soil. I'm interested in all of them, but particularly the latter. The tunnel network allows water and oxygen into the soil and allows carbon dioxide to get out. Earthworm casts (their poo) helps create the fine, crumb-like structure of a really good soil. Add to this that earthworms help process dead leaves and decomposing matter like compost or manure, and you can see why any gardener would want them.

But there's still a way to go on this soil for the worms and me. The ground feels claggy, clay-like, lumpen and, worst of all, it remains grey. James and I stare at it forlornly. Sharp sand, he advises. I drive to the nearest supplier and lug two sacks of the stuff back then empty them into the soil. It will give extra drainage, but it still looks awful, just in a different, unnaturally yellow way. Restoring this sorry patch of soil to something rich, fertile and alive is going to take me years. Essentially, this is the foundation stone of all that I am doing, and something that we can all do. I put in a call to my horse-riding chum with lots of manure. Is there any more that's well-rotted? There is. I plan my next visit.

In the rush of modern life, it's entirely possible not to touch the natural world, of which we are just another part; not to feel the wind on your face; or know where your food came from or the work that went into producing it. A signal pleasure on the allotment is that all this changes. Everything is about the soil, nurturing it and the creatures that live in it (or should do). If information is power, the best piece of information a vegetable grower can be given is a new location of well-rotted horse manure.

On a daily basis I am touching the soil, investigating it, praying for its recovery and flourishing, finding it sources of nutrients. I keep a weather eye out for not just worms, but all the invertebrates that live within the soil. When I see them,

I rejoice. This is where a meal starts, not with a menu in a Michelin-starred restaurant, or your local pub, or buying the same food every week from the supermarket. Being able to eat is the end result of nurture and care of the soil. Knowing this and contributing to it transforms your mindset.

I plant the broad beans in a square: three plants each way. The twigs support them. I water them in and hope they truly are tough enough to survive the weather and the far-from-perfect soil. That night there is a frost. I worry that they will have perished. But no, they are absolutely fine and, by the end of the month, are basking in spring sunshine and have tripled in height.

The tomatoes and flowers in the propagator at home have also shot up and I learn a lot about how not to pot them on, by picking them up by their stems, which promptly break. I watch Monty Don, on *Gardeners' World*, picking them up by their leaves and supporting them with a pencil as my father used to do, and curse myself for forgetting this. In the end, I have a smattering of tomato seedlings and fewer flowers, which can be taken to the greenhouse at the allotment to grow.

My father was obsessed with his greenhouse. He was there early and late, fiddling about with seedlings, giving them the tiniest drops of water from an elegant, old, copper watering can. He was obsessed with the greenhouse's temperature. Was it hot enough, or too hot? He created an inner sanctum made of clear plastic sheeting for his most precious seedlings, to give them the best chance of keeping warm and growing fast. He heated the greenhouse with a lightbulb powered by a car battery. Wherever he was, he wanted to get back to the green-house. Every aspect of life, it felt, was cut short in order for him to return to the greenhouse and his seedlings.

I resented it. But now I find that I've taken on his mantle. In mid-March, we get past Storms Freya, Gareth and Hannah and find ourselves in unfamiliar territory. High pressure lies over the country. It is warm for the time of year (13 degrees), sunny and still. After work one day, I pop into the allotment to see how my seedlings are doing: the first bad sign that I'm morphing into my father. It is 28 degrees in the greenhouse and the little seedlings are a bit thirsty. The next day I go after work to water them again, telling myself the while that they will be fine, that I don't need to go. I do. They wouldn't have been.

After a long day of back-to-back meetings, while I am cross-eyed with tiredness, I go again.

There is help at hand, in the slender, dark-haired form of Geordie. When I took on this plot, he did lots of the hard work, digging soil that was as hard as concrete, helping move and erect the greenhouse. He did it out of kindness and isn't afraid of hard work. 'I like creating order out of chaos,' he said. A year on, and the whole thing has become seductive. He has joined the allotment throng, working a massive plot slightly uphill from me. So now Geordie and I are running a shift system. He opens the greenhouses in the morning, I shut them after work. We have become watchful of each other's greenhouses, as well as their contents. Having dismantled and erected mine over a series of tortuous days, we know just how fragile and precious they are, and we are determined that they should survive the winter and be the scene of growth and fecundity.

Geordie's greenhouse – a more conventional oblong shape – takes a few knocks as winds buffet the door ajar, and this leads to panes of glass shattering. He replaces them with polycarbonate and finds a way to keep the door shut.

But for weeks now, we've been checking for damage on each other's plots whenever we are there. Opening windows is the next stage of the greenhouse game. The shift system will be critical in the summer, but it's already very important because the temperatures drop so much at night. By the third sunny day it is 30 degrees in my greenhouse at 9.30 a.m. I open the clearly insufficient window and leave the door ajar with bricks. Like my father, I will be here before and after work. Given that I get up at 6 a.m. to go to work, this is going to impact my day and, more crucially, my sleep. But there is something quite wonderful about seeing the little seedlings that have survived manhandling choosing to live and beginning to grow. I am in a state of disbelief that the tomato plants will actually survive, but later, tougher additions to the throng, such as cucumbers and squashes, are all looking small, but robust. Hope is already in the air.

My first full growing season: what a thought. Years ago, on an ill-fated reporting trip to Ethiopia from which I returned full of tropical diseases, we drove out into the mountains for a day's interviews. At its end, I had a long, really interesting conversation with a local man about where our respective food came from. He grew all of his and thus was self-sufficient, though at the mercy of the weather and climate change. I bought all of mine and so was at the mercy of a long food chain, the weather, climate change and supermarkets. It seemed to us both that he had the better deal, though he would have been considered poor and I comparatively rich. 'I had no idea that people bought their food,' he said, mystified. I explained the absence of land, that many people didn't even have gardens, let alone space for vegetables or animals. He looked utterly perplexed.

His response may have been a galvanizing force, on the quiet. I don't want to be dependent on supermarkets and their toneless, seasonless uniformity, their price cutting and failure to invest in British farmers. I want fresh food in season, and I want to grow it.

Supermarkets dominate the food scene in Britain. The Big Four (Tesco, Asda, Sainsbury's and Morrisons) had more than 73 per cent of the market in 2015. The discounters, Aldi and Lidl, took a further 8 per cent, with Waitrose adding 5 per cent. That's 86 per cent of the food market taken up by the supermarkets. While all our supermarkets hereabouts give grants for community projects, it feels like the balance isn't right.

They didn't always have this dominance. Sainsbury's is the oldest, dating back to 1869, when it was just a family-run grocery store. Morrisons is pretty similar, founded in 1899. But 50 years ago, it was the norm to shop locally. Supermarkets have really taken off this century. In just six years, between 2004 and 2010, the Big Four were given permission for 480 stores in England, 67 in Scotland, 22 in Wales and 8 in Northern Ireland, according to a study by *Panorama* and the BBC. Separate Ordnance Survey research showed that, in certain postcodes, the number of new stores rose during those years, by more than 700 per cent. I'd like a quiet word with the planners, frankly.

To buy from a supermarket is undoubtedly convenient. But though the prices may be low, there is no such thing as cheap food. Whenever you pick up a bargain, you have to ask yourself: who's paying for you to have that low price? As you answer that question, you can lay your bets that the benefactor won't be the supermarket. It will be the producer. That's a man or woman somewhere in the UK, working hard to grow anything from cauliflowers to strawberries, to produce bacon, cheese or milk.

Let's take milk as an example. In 2015, it cost farmers 62p to produce a 2-litre bottle of milk. They were being paid 48p per litre, less than the cost of production. How were they meant to survive? Why would supermarkets even do this? How can they not feel utterly ashamed? Before you get totally outraged, remember that the retailer then marked up the price of milk by a further 46p and the average sale price was 94p. You can conserve some of your outrage for that.

As I write, 2 litres of milk costs £1.09 in Tesco and Morrisons, £1.10 in Sainsbury's and Asda. But this isn't cause for celebration. Half of Britain's dairy farmers have gone out of business in the last ten years. Half. That's people's lives changed irrevocably, and the countryside altered, animals gone to slaughter. Ask yourself: where is the milk coming from now? Could it perhaps be somewhere with lower welfare standards? It will undoubtedly be somewhere further away, involving more food miles to get it to us.

Enough. The principles that lie behind doing this with milk imbue the whole of the supermarket system, whatever community grants are dispensed. It is the embodiment of greed and meanness. I can't keep my own cow (yet), but I can grow my own vegetables. I make a silent pledge that never again will I buy a lettuce or cucumber wrapped in plastic from a supermarket. I'm buying milk from a local goat owner. The Big Four may be more powerful than I am. But I can and will grow my own vegetables. And if I can do it (and I'm presuming that I can), then anyone can. Perhaps I can encourage others to grow a few things. We can develop a taste for change. We do not have to play the supermarkets' game and conspire with their greed and treatment of others. In this context, having a few cucumber seedlings growing, albeit slowly, in the greenhouse is a quiet form of protest. It's also achievable whoever we are. I am not Barbara Good from *The Good Life*. I'm just a middle-aged woman trying to walk along a new path. And an allotment isn't necessary to start change: a few pots of tomatoes on a patio, lettuce and herbs on a kitchen windowsill, a sack of potatoes on a balcony, all make a difference.

The slightly mind-blowing aspect of all this is that I can grow anything I want. If it doesn't work, if a plant dies, all I've lost is a few seeds. I can try again. The limits to my ambition are the soil (some plants won't like sitting in clay), the amount of rain, wind and sun, the frosts and my imagination. My imagination requires peas, as they were a staple part of my childhood diet, and sweetcorn, on the basis that surely it has to taste nicer than the shop-bought produce. I sow the seeds.

What's growing on the shelves in the greenhouse represents hope over expectation; after all, I've not done this before. But there are pots with Japanese greens, chamomile, sweet peas, morning glory, borage, red basil, plum tomatoes, celery and tromboncino. The latter are squash that look like giant marrows crossed with boomerangs. They hold their shape too. So if you cut a bit off (and you'll never eat one at once, as they're easily

2 feet long), you can leave the rest in the fridge and it won't collapse, as a courgette or marrow would. It's a random list of things to grow, but potentially no more random than anyone else's list. And it's just the beginning. By the end of May, I'll have sown far more seeds, and this, I realize, will continue through the summer, so that plans laid now will yield crops right through until this time next year. Fare ye well, Tesco.

Of course, what I don't see coming is the coronavirus pandemic. A year on we'll be locked down and there will be a huge rise in demand for allotments. Fears over food security, the desire to be outside and a dawning realization that we've only got one planet, so we'd better look after it, will drive people to grow their own food.

As I'm sowing my little seeds of hope, I'm one of some 27 million Britons who garden regularly. But lockdown will see a rise of 147 per cent in the amount of time people spend gardening. If you're not commuting, you have time to grow. Both the Royal Horticultural Society and the National Vegetable Society will report that thousands more people are gardening, particularly growing vegetables, for the first time.

Allotment sites will be inundated with requests from would-be new growers. Ours will suddenly have a 27-strong waiting list, from virtually nothing at this stage. People will phone asking: 'Can I have an allotment, just for lockdown?' Thirty-six per cent of local councils will say that they plan to increase the number of allotments available, prioritizing giving space for growing. There are already 1.9 million allotments in Britain. There will be more. Even in a pandemic, there will be hope: the hope that comes as people realize that growing vegetables isn't difficult, that they can provide for their own table, that it is delicious, that they are part of the planet's ecosystem and can contribute to it, and in the doing of that, they can take back a tiny amount of control of their lives, which feel as if they're in freefall.

For now, all that lies ahead, and the hope I have within me is the singular hope of a person embarking on a new adventure. This is no longer a theory. Seeds are in the soil. There will be plants. There will be something to eat.

APRIL

Care

April feels like it's officially spring, especially when the sun comes out and it's possible to shed some layers of winter clothing. But it isn't. April is a deeply deceptive month: warm and sunny by day, with destructive frosts at night. This means that care and attention have to be at the top of my agenda. I have to pay attention to what's actually happening on the plot, rather than what I think might be, and take care of the plants in the way that they need.

With a greenhouse full of growing seedlings and varying temperatures and weather, caring for the plants becomes a part-time job. I'm spending more than 17 hours a week at the allotment. It's never enough. But it's vital. Do this well and the plants will flourish. Overwater, underwater, water erratically, and I'll have problems and so will the plants.

This is not something that can be done in a hurry. It requires attention, stepping aside from the busyness of life, and it repays you many times over. But isn't it hard to step aside from the busyness? I find it so. And, in a way, I've just created more busyness by taking on an allotment. There is a sense in which

I'm becoming the Sorcerer's Apprentice, running hither and yon, always behind, never keeping up.

But there's another sense in which I'm learning to care, learning the importance of stopping working, stopping being concerned about myself and my life, turning aside from the endless to-do list. My level of care is a life-and-death issue for the seedlings. It's not just about popping into the allotments after work; at least it's not if you're a young tomato plant. Perspective is an interesting thing.

At the same time as trying to develop the allotment, I'm overseeing the creation of a garden at the RHS Chelsea Flower Show. It's a marked change from 33 years of reporting, but has been born out of it. If you've spent decades pitching story ideas to editors, coming up with ideas and pitching them is the stuff of life. I'm a big fan of the RHS Chelsea Flower Show. The gardens transport you to another place, inspire you and open up vistas of possibility. They also, often, tell stories. So it was that I pitched the idea of exhibiting a garden, based on Psalm 23, to the Bible Society. They said 'yes' and my life took a rather marvellous handbrake turn. Instead of trying to sell news stories to increasingly young national newspaper news editors, I'm in charge of a project whose aim is to inspire community gardens – themed on the famous psalm – around the country. At this point, I don't know that we'll be overtaken by a pandemic, that the Show will be cancelled and the garden will be held over until the following year, at best. For now, we're motoring, planning photo shoots and filming days and submitting the idea of the garden to the RHS.

This is a country mile from my old day job as a journalist. At first it felt completely alien, even though it was my idea. I was so far out of my depth that I couldn't see the bottom. To mix my metaphors, I felt like Mr Benn walking through the door of the dressing-up shop into another world, in which he would have adventures but didn't truly belong. Now, I feel as if I've come home. I'm utterly fulfilled, rushed off my feet, exhilarated and throwing my weight into doing it as well as I can.

Luck is on my side. The Psalm 23 Garden is being designed by Sarah Eberle, the most-decorated garden designer, and built by Mark Gregory, the most-decorated landscaper. They are, an RHS staffer says to me, 'A-listers', and so I am whizzing along holding on to their coat-tails, and confident in the fact that the garden couldn't be in more capable hands.

Sarah and I have become firm friends, and she's clearly pretty good for a spot of gardening advice. She takes one look at the multi-sided greenhouse and says, 'Do you have trouble controlling the temperature in that?' I fold up laughing, because clearly that's the problem. 'Is it either boiling or freezing?' she asks. It is.

Over the winter, the greenhouse has been insulated with bubble wrap. It serves to protect the seedlings from overnight frosts. Generally. But now, it can be 19 degrees in the day, and the little seedlings wilt in the heat. So Geordie and I are trying to stay one step ahead of the temperatures, opening our greenhouses up in the morning, closing them at the end of the afternoon, but hanging on to the bubble wrap just in case.

I've already learned that doing anything else can mean death. One particularly warm day was followed by a bitterly cold night. I'd removed some of the bubble wrap, and what happened? The tallest, bravest of the tomato seedlings was caught by the frost and died.

It's not just the seedlings that need protection from the frost. So does the Victoria plum tree, which is now in full bloom, a cheerful, exuberant whiteness of hope. But a week of frosts are forecast and I have no clue how to protect it. You can't bubble-wrap a tree. In my ignorance, all I can do is pray and hope that the tree will be festooned with plums in midsummer.

What does all this actually mean? Growing vegetables stops you looking inward, stops you believing your own press release, the story about yourself that you like to portray to others; your own Facebook post, if you prefer. You stop being the centre of your own world.

I was never a famous TV journalist, but I was an often-published print journalist. So that meant that, if you read certain national newspapers and magazines, you'd have seen my name in print. Having reported for years, I was in the fortunate position of being able to pick up the phone to various news and features desks and for them to know who I was, listen to my idea and, like as not, commission it. That makes it sound easy. It wasn't. It was like the north face of the Eiger most days. But the story, and my telling of it (whatever it was), was always the most important thing to me: it was all-consuming.

Friendships, potential relationships, actual relationships, holidays, sleep, exercise, fun, were all sacrificed on the altar of telling the story. I have no regrets. There's probably no more interesting, legal, way to earn a living. But I'd quite like to have a life now as well as bylines, and the seedlings are giving me that life. Occasionally, I still look ruefully over my shoulder at those of my chums who remain in the business: people with bylines, impressive job titles on national newspapers or TV stations. I have a twinge of regret. One of them – among the most daunting and frighteningly capable – says, 'You're the one with the nice life, Hazel.' Thanks to the seedlings, I think this might be true. There's more to my life than work, even though that work is now consumed by the RHS Chelsea Flower Show.

Whatever our situation, it's an easy trap to fall into: finding fulfilment in who we outwardly are, our jobs or status. But the plum tomato and celery seedlings don't care that I've written for the *Daily Telegraph*, they just want me to look after them. My care of them is life or death. What I do outside of that is completely irrelevant. That also changes who I am. I'm not a former writer for the *Daily Telegraph*, I'm an allotment holder, a carer of the soil, an encourager of plants, the custodian of a small plot of land. Instant news has been replaced by long-term investment.

As I feel the soil in the pots, checking for moisture; as I water, sow more seeds, pot the biggest plants on, I take my eyes off myself and find what was always true: that in nurturing and caring, I am fulfilled and cared for in return.

The allotment animals who live further along the rutted track also need twice-daily care. Their owners are distinct from the rest of us due to their early-morning and late-afternoon arrivals, bearing food and water. Most of the animals are now at the end of the allotments on grazing plots, in large measure to try to draw the rats away from the gardening plots. But the anomaly are the goats. Large, creamy and long-haired, they are immensely docile and friendly. I greet them every time I pass, and they gaze up at me, chewing, gentle, benign. They inhabit a large plot on the left on the way into the allotments, grazing, and often simply lying in the sun watching people walk past, hoping (one suspects) for a treat. At night, they inhabit a tumbledown wooden barn, with a sagging roof. But all day long they are by their fence-line, a welcome, cheering sight as you arrive.

On 1 April, the goats are nowhere to be seen. Perhaps they've been rehomed, or are in a different field, I think to myself. But as I leave, a youngish, fair-haired man is knocking down the fencing around their plot. The goats were sent to the abattoir today, he says. One was 15, the other 12. It was time for them to go, he adds, unable to look me in the eye.

He and his wife are divorcing. Their nearby house is to be sold. Everyone is moving. He's giving up his allotment. The goats, it would seem, fell victim to the divorce settlement. They were just one more thing to be sorted out, along with the CD collection and the furniture, before the inevitable parting.

It must have been utterly dreadful for him. A terrible decision. But there's something fundamentally heartbreaking about this, that goats should die because a couple are divorcing. We've all heard tales like it before: dogs put to sleep so a family can go on holiday; cats left behind when people move. Our care of the other occupants of this planet says a lot about us and may well shape our future as a species. As I write this, a report from the World Wildlife Fund reveals that biodiversity is being lost 'at an alarming rate'. It reveals that global populations of mammals, birds, fish, amphibians and reptiles has plunged by, on average, 68 per cent between 1970 and 2016. Sixty-eight per cent. 'This loss affects our own health and well-being,' the reports authors write. 'Today, catastrophic impacts for people and the planet loom closer than ever.'

We are so disconnected from the planet that we can't see what we're doing to it. The goats are part of this. Could we, the other plot holders, not have looked after them? I'd have done it in a heartbeat. But, in truth, I've never seen the fair-haired man before, so how could he know to ask me? Life, though, has to be a better option than death, doesn't it? A small amount of rage bubbles up inside me that this was the only option. We all loved them. Death really needn't have been the answer.

The solace I normally gain from the allotment is gone on this day. I loved those goats, and their benign, friendly faces. I loved the fact that the allotments had goats at all. It's simultaneously eccentric and real. It was a connection to the wider world of this planet, which now, in this instance has gone.

But April calls me onward out of my sadness. It is a time to look forward, a time to plant. It may be too cold for the seedlings to emerge from their greenhouse home, but the herbaceous border can be planted up. Rachel comes to lend a hand.

The principle with the border, as with any other element of allotment holding, is that buying plants is an absolute last resort. I've grown some plants from cuttings. Fran divided her own herbaceous perennials to give to me, and a few plants are being rehomed from my back garden, plants in pots that haven't been thriving. My mother donates a buddleia, also in a pot, looking sick: I'm not sure if it'll be a blessing or a curse, but it will attract butterflies. However, I have bought two climbing roses to run along the fence-line, and a good stock of bulbs: alliums, crocus and tulips. Rachel has been growing me a few more plants in her garden 15 miles away. So, on a cold, leaden-grey April day that promises nothing, we stand in front of serried ranks of pots, and plan. This is the fun bit that you see Monty Don and Alan Titchmarsh do on TV, placing plants and then standing back to see what works, moving things around until you've got it right.

This would be a whole lot easier if I could remember what I've got. We phone Fran to find out what colours the flowers are and how tall the plants. Then, slightly the wiser, we do the Monty Don thing, placing plants where we think they might look nice, creating impact with colour. We do this with no colour and only a wing-and-a-prayer hope that we're getting it right.

For me, creating a herbaceous border on clay is like entering a foreign country. I need a guidebook to tell me how things work. A mile away, at home, I've gardened on a rich, black, chalky loam for 25 years. I'm primed to buy the right plants for that setting: salvias, peonies, roses, alliums, sedum and hydrangea. It's a cottage garden in a sea of blues, purples and creams.

This will not do here, says Rachel. Clay requires daisy-like flowers: asters, dahlias, chrysanthemums, coreopsis, rudbeckia and cosmos. Immediately, we're away from the muted pallet of colours and into showier, more jewel-like tones. This border will be cheery and quite possibly gaudy. Initial disappointment that I must leave the familiar behind me gradually becomes excitement at the thought of doing something new. My comfort zone is only a mile away. I can still plant in it. But here, I am afforded the opportunity of creating something entirely fresh and different.

Rachel steps easily into the head gardener role, and I pass things and say, 'Yes, you're right,' whenever I'm asked anything. 'You need a splash of colour at the gate,' she says, setting down pots of seeming nothingness that will give me yellow, red, purple, blue and lilac all in one hit: a showstopper of an entrance way.

The divided asters come next. Tall, purple ones with yellow centres stand at the back, with diminutive darker ones grouped at the front. Roses (coral and yellow) are set to grow along the fence-line. Rachel rolls her eyes at the pink peony and tries to hide it behind other things. Once we've stood back and looked at nothing (me), the future (Rachel) a number of times, and tweaked the layout of the pots, we finally plant. First, the bulbs, which turn out to be sacrificial: nothing can survive the double whammy of squirrels and wet clay; then the plants. And in less than half an hour, it's done. The herbaceous border is ready for its first year.

The immensely satisfying bit about all this is that, until six months ago, this was grass. Worse, it was couch grass: invasive, dismal and no good for anything except providing a root system where baby worms can go to nursery during the day. But lawns are barren places, and they're remarkably bad for the environment.

In the USA, a third of all water is used maintaining lawns. Americans use nearly 9 billion gallons of water a day – yes, every day – so that's a lot of water that could be conserved and used for other things. Grass may look nice, and I appreciate that views are strong on this, but it provides virtually no habitat for pollinators or other animals. So while the herbaceous border is currently just a triangle of slowly improving clay dotted with plants, it will be home to all manner of insects, butterflies, moths and other pollinators come the summer. They will bring in the birds, and in time, one can only hope for mammals other than the resident rats.

Then we sit back and drink tea out of flasks and enjoy the glow of a job well done. I wouldn't have the allotment at all without Rachel, or indeed Fran and Geordie. All have quietly encouraged me without saying anything. They've simply got alongside me, over the years, gardened with me, and in so doing have shown me that gardening is something that anyone can do. They have metaphorically run behind me on my bicycle until I could no longer feel their hands on my back, pushing. Gardening doesn't require fantastically in-depth knowledge, just a little time, patience and enthusiasm. You have to be willing to learn from your mistakes and find time to sit and ponder.

Fran is a head gardener, and dauntingly capable. I'm never going to be as good at gardening as she is. In fact, I'm never going to be as good as she is at most things, save writing for newspapers. It was easy, therefore, to think that I couldn't really garden at all, certainly without advice from Fran, Will or Bill: my three longstanding professional horticultural chums. Not so, Rachel has said, endlessly, and Fran agreed. You can garden. You are gardening. You don't need help. You can do this. And suddenly, I seem to believe them. Yes, Rachel is helping me plant up the herbaceous border. But I know that I can do this allotment lark week-in, week-out, with the stabilizers off.

Everyone needs a friend like Rachel, Fran and Geordie: a friend who enables them to be their best, to fulfil their potential, to enjoy things that seem daunting, to flourish. We can all do so much more with the care and support of our friends, and also our neighbours and colleagues, if we allow them in.

I can sniff on the air that my fellow allotment holders are, in the main, enablers too. It's like a village, and in any small community there will be ragged relationships, a few unpleasant words, small annoyances, people who appear to be from another planet. But overall, here, we have a group of individuals working separately towards a common goal, and therefore willing to help each other in it.

While the evenings are, finally, beginning to lengthen, our day is done. Rachel packs up her cleaned tools into the back of her car and heads for home. I lock up, glance around me, and feel deeply satisfied: change is being wrought on this little plot. The herbaceous border won't rival Kew Gardens. But it will bring me joy, and that's enough.

'Endurance comes with age,' said the Rt Revd Michael Scott-Joynt, former Bishop of Winchester. In my old life as a religious affairs reporter, interviewing bishops and having the inside track on what was happening in the Church was my beat.

Bishop Michael was like the Duracell bunny. He could work and work. I was in my mid-thirties and no shirker but I couldn't understand his resilience. Where did it come from? This was his answer: 'Endurance comes with age.' It hasn't proved true for me. Tasks that involve lots of physical heft, or endurance, really aren't up my street. And one of them lies ahead. Mulching.

Mark Merritt has returned with more mulch: fresher, chunkier stuff to add depth to the paths, and the more well-rotted stuff to put on the beds to enrich the soil. I'm already seeing plenty of worms and millipedes, so I know that the winter's manure is working, but more is needed and will be for years if this unloved soil is to turn into something beautiful and fertile, a habitat for invertebrates and a larder for me.

There are two daunting mounds of mulch at the top of the path and just me and a wheelbarrow. Hours pass. Rain falls. Sun shines. If this is to be completed before the growing season begins in earnest, I need the care of my friends. Rachel returns out of sympathy. How much quicker it is to work together. She fills the wheelbarrow. I lay the path. More time passes. More tea is drunk. And suddenly, it's done. With that, the structure of the plot really comes to life. It was a barren wasteland of weeds, brambles and couch grass. Now, it's like a French potager, with its herbaceous border, two vegetable plots and two fruit plots, a shambles of water butts and a slightly leaning, jauntily coloured shed, with the greenhouse and compost bins nestled in the corner. It's enormously satisfying, as creating anything invariably is, whether that's baking a cake or knitting a jumper, laying a patio or decorating your own home. But there isn't much time to bask in that sense of satisfaction, because the second daunting mound of mulch is calling my name.

The allotments empty out over winter. Many established allotment holders are like migratory birds: they're off when the cold weather arrives, returning in the spring for another season. Over the winter, the allotments have been left to a few die-hard old gents who spend every morning pottering about and drinking coffee, and those of us who are trying to establish our plots.

James and Nikki – who can make anything out of anything – have been erecting greenhouses, installing a serious rainwater collection system and putting up the biggest brassica cage I have ever seen. Brassicas (cabbages, kale, Brussels sprouts etc.) aren't inherently bad. They don't need caging as punishment, merely to protect them from the cabbage white butterfly, which loves to lay its eggs on their leaves. The resultant horde of caterpillars can shred your plants overnight, as I'll later discover. Brassicas are also much beloved of pigeons. Leave them uncovered and, overnight, the pigeons will take every fragment of leaf, meaning that you are greeted with a stalk in the morning. So some kind of cage is important. James' could keep the Foreign Legion out.

James keeps a weather eye on my struggles, and when he can bear my lack of skill no longer, invariably walks over and offers to help. So it is that he sees me weary of the second mound with which I'm mulching the raspberry bed. He walks over, takes the wheelbarrow and shovel and goes back and forth with six loads of mulch, covering half of the raspberry bed. This kind of care makes the difference between coping and giving up. He smiles: 'Don't be daft,' and returns to the brassica cage.

'A little bit of help is worth a lot of pity,' my grandmother said. She was right. James' six loads of mulch gives me a break and enables me to gather myself for the last push. Time passes and the well-rotted mulch pile decreases. The colour of the soil improves. I do my 10,000 steps a day and several other people's. Finally, there's nowhere else to put any mulch, and the fun bit begins: giving the rest away.

We are hard-wired in today's Britain to sell, to work for money, to know the value of everything. Car boot sales and internet sales have replaced bring-and-buy stalls. So one of the allotments' great pleasures is its circular economy. You will be given all manner of things that you have not bought. Looking back, I've been given seedlings (leeks, cauliflowers, lettuces, cabbages, cavolo nero, tomatoes), seeds (black beans, lentils, runner beans, broad beans) and then the produce itself (apples, courgettes, marrows, squashes, tomatoes, chillies, lettuce ... the list is endless). The more you give away yourself, the more likely you are to be a recipient of others' generosity. People like to give back, so give first, and who knows what you'll get in return. So I eye the pile of mulch, thrilled that no more shovelling needs to be done on my part, and look around for likely recipients.

Geordie is the first. He's helped me from day one, when the soil was like concrete, digging for hours and smiling and saying that he was enjoying it. He and I also lived through the trauma of greenhouse relocation. So he is first choice for the gift of mulch. His vast, Instagram-able plot is diagonally opposite mine, up the hill. He has a fine view of the cricket and football pitches, as well as the hills beyond, if he ever sat down on his wine terrace to look at it. Would he like some mulch? He assuredly would. Immediately, in case the offer is withdrawn, he starts barrowing loads up to his plot. His soil was cared for by the previous occupants (unlike mine), but he won't turn down free mulch to keep improving it.

Next are my immediate neighbours. They are archaeologists and are always away digging holes somewhere during the summer months, which is, frankly, a bit odd for allotment holders, as summer is the growing season. So they're only ever around in the spring and autumn. To cope with this, they have a very neat little plot with raised beds, making growing their own fruit and veg easier to manage. The paths in between the beds are looking a little tired. Would they like some mulch? They fall on my neck with joy. And before I can turn around, the menacing pile of mulch has gone and the work is done.

The spirit of giving is truly upon us by now and we're all giving each other whatever we can. There's a rather grim storage unit in my shed which I absolutely do not want. Would my friends Barbara and Garry like it? They would. Off it goes. They're happy and I am thrilled, as space is gained in the shed for what I actually need. There are also seeds that I no longer want, so I give them away too. In return, the archaeologists give me a bucketful of Swiss chard for the hens, James fixes my shed door (which I hadn't noticed was broken) and Barbara brings me a traditional Portuguese cake: almost as good as the ones she has at home, she says.

It is early days for me at the allotment, so I'm still prone to buying things, rather than bartering or asking around. Time and experience change that. I learn the basic allotment holder's etiquette: whenever offered anything, say yes. It is the height of rudeness to turn down an offer. Plus, you may never be offered anything again.

Barbara – beautiful, with long wavy dark hair, a million-candle smile and a kind heart – is offered everything by everyone. It's almost comical. In our second year, we sit one summer's day as she plants out French beans (given by a neighbour and left in a bucket for three days). They look on the point of death, but it's worth a try, says Barbara. And of course, they flourish.

'I am so behind,' she says. This is the mantra of just about everyone, so generally worth ignoring. 'No, really, I am,' she says. 'I have nothing to plant out for the winter. What am I going to do?'

'Oh, I don't know,' I say. 'It'll sort itself out.' And it does. By that September, we're having another break, another cup of tea, and she shows me what's happened. There are serried ranks of leeks, cabbages, purple sprouting broccoli and Brussels sprouts. There's enough to feed a large family, not just Barbara and Garry.

'I thought you didn't have anything?' I say. 'I didn't,' she laughs. 'All these plants were given to me, and the netting that's gone over them too.'

Being young, beautiful, winning, with a million-candle smile helps when it comes to being given things. But the circular economy of the allotments applies to us all, old, young and the distinctly middle-aged. A lot of it is luck. Are you in the right place when someone decides they no longer need their poly-tunnel, strimmer, netting, seedlings or seeds? But luck or no, it's a lesson in holding things lightly, sharing, and indeed giving away everything that you don't need. By the end of the second summer, I'll have got a proper handle on this, giving seedlings to many of my neighbours at home, encouraging them to grow their own vegetables, taking armfuls of vegetables back to the street and offering them to whoever wants them: piles of cucumbers, tomatoes and, endlessly, courgettes. But for now, this is an early foray into a different way of thinking: don't hold on to things, give them away, and like the bread on the waters, they will come back to you. That is a very uplifting feeling indeed.

I had thought that having an allotment was about growing vegetables. Now, I realize that this is a by-product of what it's genuinely about. So, one evening, Geordie, his partner, Kate, and I are sharing a bottle of wine, and Kate bemoans the fact that Geordie is now, like me, at the allotments an awful lot. 'It really can't take that long to grow vegetables, can it?' she says.

It's not about vegetables, I say. It's about improving the soil, connecting with the planet, with the immediate nature all around you. It's about giving and receiving, being part of a community, creating something from nothing, working with the seasons and the weather and being shaped by the process. It's about going beyond yourself and reaching out to God in his creation. It's about understanding your place in the scheme of things, being truly grateful for your food, barely ever going to the supermarket, eating seasonally, creating your meals based on what you have, giving away your surplus, reaping what you didn't sow, stopping and looking, planning and thinking, endlessly digging and mulching; and just occasionally, it's about vegetables.

She looks slightly taken aback. 'That was a passionate speech,' she says. 'Well,' I say, 'I feel passionately about it.' I do. And it's only April. What will come next?

MAY

Crazy Busyness

The little many-sided greenhouse is groaning at the seams. Seeds start life grown in tiny 'plugs', or in rows in a broad tray. Once they're up and have their first pair of proper leaves (not just their baby ones), they'll reach the point of just sitting and sulking unless you pot them up; that is to say, plant them into a bigger pot. This has to happen several times to take a tiny seedling an inch high to the point where it's a sufficiently big and strong plant to go outside.

Though the greenhouse came with shelving all the way round, I'm only using it on one side, to allow me to have a few tomatoes and cucumbers in large pots in the rest of the space as summer progresses. Currently, this means that the seedlings are crammed on to shelves like commuters on the Underground at rush hour.

The earliest to be planted (tomatoes, aubergines, peppers, chard and cabbages) are now a decent size, and stand smartly on the top shelf reaching towards the sun. But I've also planted the allotment thugs (courgettes, squash, pumpkins, cucumbers and a selection of beans). These are so fast-growing that you can virtually stand and watch them grow. Certainly, every day they are bigger than the day before. And that means they are vying for space on the top shelf, where there's more room to grow. Move them up there and everything else will suffer as they will stick their metaphorical elbows out and take all the light. So, for now, we have the Underground at rush hour.

But it's time to add to the ranks: purple sprouting broccoli, sweetcorn grown in toilet rolls, leeks in old grape containers, and more lettuce. Small plants arrive in the post: bergamot and stevia, as I dream up a fantasy that I might be able to make my own Earl Grey tea and sweeten it with stevia instead of sugar. They're a bit battered after their journey and need a few days' convalescence in the warmth of the greenhouse Underground before being planted outside. Where is everything to go? There are seedlings all over the floor of the greenhouse and on thrown-together shelving made of planks of wood and old bricks. It's not pretty, but it does the job.

It took me a while to learn that, when a seedling stopped growing, it needed more room. Asking, 'Why aren't you growing?' didn't prove particularly effective. Continuing to water simply kept the plant alive. Light dawned. You need more space to grow, more nutrients, and then you'll flourish.

There are times in our own lives that are like this, but they can be harder to recognize. Been in the same job for too long? Afraid to move? Got annoying neighbours, but can't face putting your house up for sale? Is your marriage loveless but familiar? Any major change, whether it be a relationship, work or a physical move, can give us the new environment that we need to continue to flourish and become the people we were intended to be. But so often it's easier to sit where we are, like the seedlings, and grow no further.

Maybe that's fear operating. There is, after all, a risk in changing one's situation. I'm writing this in the midst of the coronavirus pandemic. Anyone with a job or a home is clinging to them like a drowning person to the wreckage of a ship. We are all waiting for our furloughs to end, or the boss to make the unpleasant announcement that we're going to be made redundant.

Perhaps you've had bosses like that – I know I have – ones who ask: 'Why aren't you doing this?' 'Why aren't you different from how you are?' Generally, this is code for 'Why aren't you more like me?' or even subliminally and perhaps unconsciously, 'Why aren't you a man?' When you have a boss like that, pandemic or no pandemic, you tend to gaze out of the window and wish that someone would give you the space to grow, the nutrients that you need to flourish, to become what you are meant to be, or perhaps simply to recognize that you're a courgette not a lettuce, and no amount of questioning is going to change who or what you inherently are.

Voluntarily looking for a new job or moving house is, in the context of a pandemic, the action of the very brave or those who are somehow impregnable to harm. However, I do know a few people who fall into the very brave category: a young couple taking the opportunity that not being fixed to a desk affords them to move out of London. I know they'll flourish in a greener setting. There's a young father who's been headhunted for a new job. He's the kind of person to have the vision for fresh experiences, and seized the opportunity with both hands, though he was sad to say farewell to his colleagues and a job he loved. And then there's my next-door neighbour. He's been made redundant and, despite an exhaustive search, can't find another role in academia. So he's creating fresh challenges for himself, casting himself on the tides of the universe and the potential adventure that this will allow him.

I am not like these people. I sit and wait for the sword of Damocles to fall. I try to take opportunities, but am cautious, and don't seize all of them. But I am able to see that, for a seedling, the opportunity to grow can only happen if I facilitate it. The seedlings just wait for me to catch on. When I do, I discover the absolute therapeutic joy of potting on. I stand in the gloom of the shed, serried ranks of small pots on the bench in front of me, with buckets of compost and a tray of seedlings. Each seedling has to be lifted gently out of its old home and placed into a new, individual pot, where it can do the next bit of its growing. An old teaspoon seems to be the best tool for the job. Gently, slowly, one seedling after another, they are potted on. You could call it boring, but I find it completely relaxing. My mind drifts away into the seedlings' future, when they'll be big strong plants producing a harvest; or to next May, when we'll be at the RHS Chelsea Flower Show. But, thankfully, my thoughts are mostly about the seedlings. I'm eating, drinking and sleeping the RHS Chelsea Flower Show by this stage. So potting on is the moment for stepping aside and not thinking about it.

'You like potting on?' my mother says, surprised. 'You must be very patient.' We both know I'm not.

There's an obvious consequence of potting on. Everything takes more space. Tiny seedlings that were crammed into plugs now have a little pot all to themselves, or a considerably bigger pot in the case of the allotment thugs. So where 30 seedlings took up 1 square foot, now they take up far more.

I try to keep them all together in trays labelled with their type: a tray for tomatoes, another for cucumbers, courgettes and so on. But this never works. After a time, inevitably, you move things around, and then the absence of individual labels on each pot rumbles you.

I spend a lot of time looking at seedlings thinking, 'You could be a courgette. But you might be a pumpkin. Or then again, you could be a butternut squash.'

The obvious answer to this is that you label every single pot. But that would be too sensible, so somehow, I don't. Instead, I am growing confusion. I'm not alone. The following summer, five of us are sitting on a neighbour's plot reflecting on how our harvest is going. 'The courgettes never stop,' says Kasia, who's from Poland, works in academia and works equally ferociously hard on her plot, accompanied by her bulldog Pepi. 'How many plants have you got?' I ask. 'Twelve,' she replies. 'Twelve?' The assembled company howls with laughter, knowing that you could supply half of Winchester with the harvest from 12 courgette plants. They're so prolific.

'I'm a bit disappointed,' says Kasia. 'I thought they'd be butternut squash plants. But I must have given all of those away. I love butternut squash, but I'm not crazy about courgettes.'

This is what happens in the May greenhouse shuffle. Barbara sends me a picture with the kind of plant labels that actually represent what's going on in our greenhouses. They read, 'Dead plant. Dead. Did I plant that? **** if I know. Not sure. Still alive. No idea. Tried and died. Probably plants. Something green. Cheaper than therapy. Plants. Not dead yet. Stayin' alive.' It's not just me then?

Regardless of what the plants may actually be, I think that a little bit of encouragement never goes amiss. So I tell them how well they're doing. At the beginning of the month, those receiving gold stars are the patty pans (courgettes that look like spaceships), tromboncino (a squash with more than a passing resemblance to a French Horn), runner beans, beef tomatoes, cucumbers and purple sprouting broccoli. A few squashes are also catching up, respectably, as one would expect. They get daily praise. Anything looking a bit feeble is told that it could do better, and that it doubtless will. I believe in it. It's alright. My greenhouse is tucked away in a far corner of the allotment. No one can hear me in here. Barbara confesses to talking to her plants too. 'They are my co-workers,' she laughs. 'It's a business meeting.'

Picture May in your mind's eye and it is sunny, balmy, warm and blue-skied. You might imagine yourself wearing summer clothes, sitting in the garden, sipping a glass of wine. The beginning of this May is the polar opposite of that. In comes the first Bank Holiday of May, a time, surely, for pottering around in the garden, doing some serious work on the allotment and spending your disposable income at the garden centre. Not this year. Instead, we have the coldest May Day Bank Holiday since 1973. It is 13.2 degrees by day and just 5 degrees at night.

Instead of summer clothing, I'm layered up in a t-shirt, jumper, jacket and a woolly hat.

There is an unexpected frost. So I'm regretting dismantling the bubble wrap that encased the greenhouse, thinking that we were past the last frosts. We aren't. The plants are regretting my decision too. Three cucumber plants are brown with frost burn and will never recover. Many seeds remain dormant in their soil, unwilling to even attempt growing until a far warmer climate is safely established.

Outside, it's carnage. Sweet peas planted out early along the fence-line have gone white with the cold. Red basil plants have wilted and died. I'm particularly sorry about those, as I bought the seeds while visiting my cousin, Laura, who lives in Venice. I returned home after a wonderful break, with a handful of seed packets, keen to sow the plants of Venice in Hampshire. I'm already learning the glaringly obvious: that the plants of Venice need to grow in Venice. They don't come prepared for the bitter chill of a British Bank Holiday weekend. I dig them out and add them to the compost heap.

The chickpeas, however, are proving hardier than one might imagine. Are all beans tough? They're now six inches tall, with frothy fronds of green growth, and are entirely captivating in their exoticness. Bible Society colleagues in Jordan cheer on my attempt to grow them, via email and Zoom. I can only hope that the chickpeas don't mind being substantially colder than they'd normally be if they were growing in the Middle East.

Having casualties is, however, the norm. Geordie (whose excellence at growing vegetables rivals only his excellence at magazine editing and cooking) has also had losses: cucumbers, squashes and tomatoes. I wander around comparing notes. Everyone, it seems, has lost their potatoes. This isn't particularly terrible as potatoes are robust. Cover the frosted brown leaves with soil, straw or hay, and the tubers will recover, sending forth new growth.

What you learn about casualties is that death isn't the end. Who knew the plot could be so spiritually enriching? In vegetable rather than human terms this means that, generally, there is time to replant. If there isn't, you can be sure that someone else will have spare plants to give you. And if all else fails, you can buy some plants.

Through this, over successive springs, I learn the concept of 'enough'. No matter how many plants die, how many seeds are eaten by the blackbirds, pigeons and squirrels, no matter how many perish in frosts, fail to thrive in hot sun, or give up in torrential rain, there will always be enough to eat. Furthermore, there will always be more than enough to eat and plenty to give away. It is utterly remarkable.

This experience changes how I view life, money and possessions. I stop clinging to what I have, fearful of loss, and, very gradually, start to believe that there will be provision. I normally want to thump Christians who say, 'God will provide.' It seems so smug, so glib, so unrelated to the lives of many. But the testament of my allotment is that indeed God does. I may not have red basil, but I do have tromboncino.

Slowly, I start to lean back and relax into the idea that there will be enough. Learning this during a pandemic has been a very interesting experience. The allotment will always give me something to eat. But the idea of enough goes beyond vegetables and touches every aspect of life. Instead of wanting more, further, bigger, better, if I am happy with enough, I will be content.

'More' – there's a problematic word. Somewhere between the rationing of post-war Britain and today, we have come to believe that having more is not only desirable, it is our right, the norm, and thus needs to be immediately fulfilled. Waiting is out of fashion. The consequences of this horrible miscalculation are all around us. According to the Money Advice Service, in 2019 some 8.3 million Britons were in debt. Twenty-two per cent of UK adults had less than £100 in savings, making them very vulnerable to financial shocks, which, of course, then came along.

This is a whole lot worse if you're young. A survey of 18–24-year-olds for the Money Advice Trust by YouGov, found that 37 per cent of young people are already in debt, owing roughly £2,989 (excluding student loans and mortgages). Fifty-one per cent report that they regularly worry about money, and 21 per cent say that they lose sleep about it.

This is a complex issue. There'll be many reasons behind these statistics. But the insidious idea of having more (stuff, money or experiences), and having it now, is a part of our culture. It is so easy to get sucked into this. What do your friends and neighbours have? That's the norm. You want it too.

I live in a Victorian terrace. When I moved in, the road was inhabited by people with trades: builders, nurses, artists, writers. The houses were all nice, but no one could afford extensive building and refurbishing work. Scroll on a couple of decades and the houses are lived in by professionals. You can't go five paces without tripping over a doctor, surgeon or vet. It's very handy if you, or your cat, are ill. The houses are now like Tardises: designed in the latest trends, looking more like five-star hotels than Victorian terraced houses.

After a while, this started to get to me. Perhaps I needed work done on my house too? After all, it lacked the glamour, the open-plan design, the triple-glazed French windows, the en-suite bedrooms of its neighbours. Did this mean I was a failure? Was I also stupid, having not earned enough money to afford this? It shone a light on my single status – and the choices that had led to that. If I had married there would potentially have been a second income to make all this en-suite and extension business possible. Should I put myself in debt to the tune of £30,000 to keep up with what others had done? A neighbour in a similar house sat me down and talked some common sense into me. 'You *live* in this house. It is your home,' she said. 'It's not an investment. Forget it.' I did. But it was a salutary lesson in how subtle the idea of 'more' is, how it creeps up on you. The allotment has brought me back to the idea of 'enough'.

The allotment facilitates the enoughness of life, through a rickety table outside a portacabin. The portacabin is the office. No one ever goes there. But the rickety table is oft-used, as it's the place for leaving anything, including any plant, that you no longer want. So it's a good place to check regularly, especially at this time of year. Tomato seedlings appear on the table. Geordie's losses are provided for. Fran gives me a couple of cucumber plants to replace the frost-burnt ones.

If there is enough – indeed, if there is more than enough – then it is possible to give away without worrying. Actually, the idea of holding on to all the plants I have is far more of a worry than giving them away. You never intend to have too many plants. But you sow more seeds than you think you'll need, expecting that some will fail to germinate, others will be frosted, others will simply dwindle and die. You allow for casualties. And still there are too many.

So I decide to take some plants into work and give them away to colleagues. This is an act of faith because I work with people who barely seem to go outside, let alone grow anything. There is general amusement and perplexity about my interest in gardening. It's not universal. I have a few like-minded work chums who build raised beds and grow carrots. But you'd hardly describe most of my colleagues as keen gardeners. I felt as if I had to snake-charm some of them into thinking that a garden at the RHS Chelsea Flower Show was a good idea.

So I load up the car with cucumber, tomato, courgette, pumpkin and butternut squash plants and drive along the M4. The office is on a soulless industrial estate. I park, beg a trolley from the estates team and lug the plants up in the lift to the first floor.

It's a vast, open-plan office. If you stand up and peer around from your desk like a meerkat, you can see most of the more than 100 staff who are in on a busy day. So bringing something unusual into the office is soon spotted. Like most workplaces, people are on a general lookout for cake, but a desk covered in plants is a reasonable second. I let it be known, through the office's intranet system, that plants are available, and soon I'm surrounded by both the few keen gardeners and those who've hardly been outdoors.

The plants change hands quickly. I give tips on how to plant and care for them. People listen to me like I'm Monty Don. I try to keep a straight face, knowing how amused both Fran and Rachel would be. I encourage weekly feeding of plants. 'Oh, that's far too complicated,' says the CEO's PA. 'You practically run this office,' I say. 'How hard is adding a bit of tomato feed to some water by comparison?' 'But I haven't

done it before,' she counters. 'When did that ever stop you?'
I say. 'Just buy some tomato feed at the supermarket next
time you're there. It's not difficult.' She mutters and walks off,
tomato plants in hand.

Am I sending the plants to an early death? It appears not. As
the summer wears on, their owners turn up at my desk with
increasing regularity. Initially, I think they're wanting to talk
about work, possibly the Chelsea Flower Show. I soon learn
that I'm in for a vegetable question: My tomato plant is a bit
floppy, what should I do? Stake it. I've got far more cucumbers
than I can eat. Give some away. Can I grow a courgette in a
pot? Not if you want courgettes. How long do I have to wait
for a pumpkin? Late September.

It's not just the questions that are new, it's the attitude too.
From almost nothing, the office has become a place where
people are interested in plants, want to grow them, believe that
they can, and get very, very excited when they do. A year later,
the CEO's PA sends me a message. We're all working from
home by this stage, so there's little chance of a chat. She sends
a photo of some tomatoes and sweet peas that she's grown – all
by herself. It's a triumph, I tell her. Well done.

We are a nation of gardeners. Some 27 million of us (that's
nearly half the adult population) garden regularly. That was
before the coronavirus hit. During lockdown, gardening was
one of the few activities open to people, so the interest in it
soared. The Royal Horticultural Society reported that in these
early months of the year, more than a third of a million people

researched how to grow potatoes, strawberries and tomatoes at home. Perhaps my colleagues are among them. And interest in the RHS's information about compost has risen by 500 per cent. With garden centres shut, online sales soared. Many suppliers of both seeds and plants had to halt sales temporarily in order to catch up with demand. Taking plants into work wasn't just about getting rid of my surplus. It was about inspiring people to feel that this was something that they could do too, and that many of them would enjoy.

One of the most cheering was Dai, a Welsh colleague. He's a poet, wonderfully creative and positive. We had lots of conversations about his back garden: a place that he didn't go because he didn't know how to deal with it. I drew designs, made suggestions, all to no avail. Then, in lockdown, he grew tomatoes. And the tomatoes fruited. He ate them, and of course, they were the most delicious tomatoes he'd ever had. The lights went on. I attended one very memorable staff meeting where Dai gave a whole presentation about his tomato plants, which he had named. I think the presentation was meant to be about something else, but I can only recall the enthusiasm about tomatoes. That may be a simple pleasure, but it's also an unalloyed joy, and open to all, whether or not you have a garden. Allotments are one of the places that people with no outside space can begin to flex their 'growing' muscles.

Allotments are dotted all around Winchester and among the outlying villages. The mothership for all of them is the Park Road allotment site, as it has, wonder of wonders, a shop. It's just a large wooden cabin, but it has everything you could possibly want at a fraction of the price that you'd pay in the stores. It has the musty, dusty smell of an old shed, and indeed motes of dust dance in the light of the few, grubby windows. It's staffed by volunteers, who all have allotments there, so it's not the kind of place to go if you're in a hurry. But if you're after a bargain and have some time to kill, it's heavenly.

I'm served by a fellow middle-aged woman. I explain that I want to make a brassica cage. 'How big?' she asks. I'm not entirely sure and so pace out the size that I think it will be. She measures it, does some sums half in her head, half out loud, and comes up with what I'll need. While she's busy measuring tubing and netting, I browse. There are shelves of home-made plant feed in old Robinson's lemonade bottles, packets of seeds for just 80p, green twine and bamboo canes. The walls are lined from floor to ceiling. I could buy the shop, and nearly do, filling the car with the brassica cage necessities and several bottles of the home-made plant feed. Perhaps I should take one in for the CEO's PA and her hungry tomatoes?

Back at the plot, James wanders over to inspect my haul. He's a veteran of the Park Road shop and approves my purchases. James loves a construction job and can explain, in detail, how it will be achieved, ending by saying, 'Easy'. So he's physically unable to walk away and leave me to it. Half an hour later, the first brassica cage is up. The pigeons will not eat my purple sprouting broccoli, whatever else they eat. It's not going to win any design awards, but it's functional: three hoops of bright blue tubing placed on bamboo canes to make an archway. That is then covered in netting, which is tied in place with string. It's a bit rickety, but every plot has them and it feels like a rite of passage. If you have a brassica cage with blue tubing, you are an allotment holder. I am a Brownie with her first badge.

Early summer has snuck up on me. By mid-May, though it is still overcast, signs of summer are all around me. For a start, I'm harvesting: rhubarb and broad beans to begin with, but now the first strawberries. Nothing from a supermarket ever tasted so good, I'm convinced.

The winter coat of weed-suppressing membrane has been removed and the bare soil is ready for its first customers: the allotment thugs. Four pumpkin plants, two patty pans and a tromboncino all make it out into the still-grey, still-clayey, but marginally more friable soil. I add to their ranks a grid of sweetcorn.

Most things you plant in rows, largely so that you can see where your plants are and what's weeds: particularly useful when everything is young and rather interchangeable. Not so with sweetcorn. It is wind pollinated, so planting it in a row would be next to useless. Plant in a grid pattern, however, and you have the chance of the wind pollinating each plant, which-ever way it's blowing.

Sweetcorn object to having their roots disturbed. The old gardeners' trick to get round this is to take a used cardboard toilet roll, make four slits at one end, bend them over outwards and thus create a base. This gives you a plantable container, as cardboard rots down in the soil. I've been saving my toilet rolls like a hoarder through the winter, and about a month ago, I filled a tray of them with soil and a sweetcorn seed each. Much to my surprise, they flourished. Now, the plants are recog-nizably sweetcorn plants – if only eight inches tall – and they too are outside, in a grid. The early bean wigwams have been erected and the beans planted at their base.

Inside the greenhouse, the allotment thugs looked like the big bruisers of the vegetable world, elbowing smaller plants out of their way in a race for the light. Once outside, they look small and vulnerable. I worry about them. We're still not past the last frosts. Is this how parents feel when they see their children go to their first day of school?

It is time for a day off. Two colleagues and I are attending the RHS Chelsea Flower Show. I think you can legitimately call this research. We're plotting, working out where the best footfall is and thus which would be the best position for the Psalm 23 Garden. Could we ask the RHS for it? Is that how it works? Probably not, but if we don't have a sense of where we'd like to be, we can't even mention it. We settle on the position we'd really like: in front of the Royal Hospital, next to some much-needed seating, alongside the Great Marquee. It is dramatic, and very tangible. I can see that my idea is about to become reality. Next year, it will be us, though of course it won't. It's a good job I don't know that yet.

The crowds are vast. Some 188,000 people visit the Show over the six days. It's a good-natured crowd, queuing patiently to get in, queuing to see each garden, queuing for the toilets, food and so on.

I'm buoyed up on a tide of excitement and possibilities. We walk round, and round again. We stop to look at Sarah Eberle's Resilience Garden. Three times. I'm trying to make the point (without saying it) that she is brilliant. Then, we bump into Sarah on her way to a TV interview. Everyone smiles. My colleagues are agog. They've met a celebrity. It's not just an idea that is talked about in meetings any longer.

If you're exhibiting a garden at the RHS Chelsea Flower Show, it's wise to hold an evening event to which you invite people with whom you want to build relationships. That can be anything, depending on your organization. Previous exhibitors have told me that people who they'd been trying to meet for months or years without success all accepted tickets to Chelsea. Relationships were forged. That's such a crucial element of any work that we're planning to do this too. So at 5 p.m., our colleague who's in charge of this turns up. It would be fair to say that he's been underwhelmed by the possibilities of Chelsea. He can't quite see the business case. Nonetheless, he's come to look round (rather proving the business case without realizing it), looking very dapper, with a white silk scarf and a straw hat. He chats away. We nod and smile, wordlessly leading him towards the plot that we'd like. He walks round the corner, sees it, and stops talking in mid-sentence. 'Wow,' he says. 'Wow,' we agree.

Everyone is now convinced that the Psalm 23 Garden is A Good Thing. It's time for my colleagues to depart, though I'm staying on for the evening. So I walk through the throngs to see them off at one of the gates. By the gate is an old-fashioned grey tractor, surrounded by plants: foxgloves and lavender. 'On you get,' says the dapper colleague. So, up I jump, in my best dress, thanking the heavens that it has a big skirt and was paired with plimsols. I smile broadly. 'You look very at home up there,' he says, taking a few photos. 'I feel it,' I say. And I know that I've come home.

JUNE

Expansion

I have found my natural milieu both at the RHS Chelsea Flower Show and also at the allotment, which is less grand, has fewer visitors, more weeds and requires considerably less expertise. It's a bit of a surprise. But both tell a story and enchant with the ideas of fresh possibilities. Both are about growth and so it perhaps shouldn't be a surprise that I'm growing too: in confidence, aspiration, hope, as well as skills. Now into June, the days are lengthening, evenings are truly with us, and so there is the possibility of spending time at the allotment after work, not just to do the bare minimum of sustaining life, but to make progress too.

Sitting at a desk, it can feel as if very little changes in the course of six months. Your colleagues are the same, the meetings are pretty similar, the work a continuation of the previous months'. Outside, on the plot, the passage of time, the march of the seasons, is far easier to see. A year ago, couch grass and brambles hid piles of rubbish. Two sheds were about to fall over. Three trees managed to sustain life, despite their surroundings, though the little apple tree later collapsed under the weight of its fruit and died. Six months ago, there were strips of bare soil where the beds were planned, patches of grass joining them, no proper paths, no new trees, no greenhouse. I could see it in my mind's eye. In reality it was nothing.

How much difference six months has made. Instead of couch grass, neatly lined woodchip paths lead to all the beds. Only one shed remains, upright, jauntily painted in blue and green, with its string of second-hand water butts storing rainwater. Where there was junk, there is now a greenhouse full of seedlings. And definition has been given by the chestnut paling fencing. This is a clearly defined space, not a jumbly, indeterminate mess.

In the big vegetable bed, purple sprouting broccoli plants seem to have more than enough room to grow under their three-hooped cage. The grid of sweetcorn, though still small, is definitely growing and actually looking like corn. Runner beans and purple climbing beans have managed to climb at least a foot up their three bamboo-cane wigwams, relieved to get their roots in the soil and start motoring.

Over on the smaller bed, more purple sprouting and curly kale are trying to work up the incentive to grow under a second three-hooped netted cage. Dwarf peas are growing well alongside them. But the real triumphs are the nurseryman's broad beans – bedecked with their distinctive white and black flowers, and now bean pods – and the metre square of chickpeas, frothily waving in the breeze. And it's always breezy at the plot, even on a still day.

Rows of onions and garlic are standing tall, their strong green leaves beginning to fade to yellow. This is a sure sign that soon they can be harvested. My own onions! A tiny pot of chives and an equally small one of marjoram have spread so much that I couldn't get my arms round them if I tried. The chives are in full, perky, purple flower, looking very pleased with themselves. They are covered in bees.

The bees don't know where to start on the formerly barren plot, but a good place is the phacelia. Under the quince and pear trees is a bed with perhaps the most awful soil of the whole area: compacted, grey and lifeless. The pressing need seemed to be to enrich it, rather than try to grow anything on it. So I opted for a green manure. These are plants which can be cut back and dug into the soil, adding much-needed nitrogen and structure to it. Phacelia is one of them.

It has a curious lilac-coloured flower head in the shape of a ponytail, borne on straggly stems. I've heard it called 'crack for bees'. I prefer to think of it as sustenance rather than a drug habit, but there's no doubt about the bees' love for phacelia. Knowing this, I abandoned the soil-improvement route and let it flower, which it has been doing for two or three weeks already. It is festooned with bees at all times of the day. And there's such a variety of bees too. I ring my friend Clare (an authority on the subject) repeatedly to ask what they all are. My favourite, and perhaps hers too, is the hairy-footed flower bee. How can you not love something with that name? The hairy-footed flower bee emerges from hibernation in February and March. It's a really important pollinator for early spring flowers. It's drawn to tubular flowers, in which it feeds using its long tongue. The males are a rusty brown, the females black, but both have long, orange hairs on their middle legs, hence the name. They like to nest in old mortar between bricks, so if you ever find a bee by a fireplace, it's probably a hairy-footed flower bee that's fallen down the chimney.

Now, it's one of the first to arrive on the phacelia and the last to leave as the sun sets. They're joined by honeybees that live in hives further along the allotments, red carder bees and tawny mining bees. The thrumming of the massed ranks of the bees can be heard anywhere on the plot and provides a gentle back-drop to my work. Add in the cawing of the rooks in the oak rookery, the starlings, pigeons, sheep bleating further up the track, Anne's geese and a couple of cockerels, and it is entirely possible to blank out the white noise of the M3. Though I'm unaware of it, others aren't. Our social media team ask me to make a little video on the plot encouraging others to send their videos of how gardening has helped them. I'm quite pleased with the results. The social media editor, however, is horrified. 'It's so noisy, Hazel,' he says. 'It's meant to be an escape, a haven, not sound like that.' Havens have many forms, I think, but don't say.

Change has been wrought in the vegetable beds, and the herbaceous border has seen massive change too: from couch grass, to manure under a layer of black membrane, to soil with a few dead sticks of divided plants breaking through the surface, all in the space of a few months. Now it looks as if it really might become a flower bed. The alliums have defied the clay soil, haven't rotted and are up and flowering. The achillea seedlings are now proper plants, and all the divisions from friends' gardens are standing 10–12 inches tall. The scabious (also grown from seed) is threatening to flower and the serried ranks of foxgloves are growing by the day.

I can see the allure of gardening television programmes in which an entire garden is created in a weekend, but they sell a myth: that a garden can be created in a weekend. It can't. Even if it could, why would you want that? This plot has only taken six months to emerge from its cocoon and start to dry off its wings in the sun. It will probably take the rest of my life to turn, fully, into what it can be, and thus to transform me too. But that's fine. That's the process. That's the joy of it. That's living and flourishing.

As I write, a new family has joined the allotments. Their large plot was a mess, but fellow allotment holders have worked hard to clear it for them. Finally, someone got the team tractor out and rotovated the ground, preparing it for the growing season. It was the best chance anyone could have: a blank slate. The smartly dressed father looked rather forlornly at the plot and said, 'I guess it's fun when it's all up together and how you like it.' 'No,' I said, 'the fun is getting it to that state. The fun is the journey.' He looked doubtful.

But by buying into the myth of the instant garden we miss so much: the planning, dreaming, decision-altering, creating, the sheer dogged chipping away at big tasks into bite-sized chunks, the warm glow of satisfaction knowing that a sturdy plant came from a seed that you sowed, and that it not only survived, but flourished. Somehow. We miss life and replace it with shopping.

We also lose any connection with, knowledge of and invest-ment in our surroundings. We may as well have walked into a film set for all the involvement that we have had in creating that space. Start from scratch, or even further back than scratch, and every inch of your land is invested in meaning. More, you understand what's going on, what the plants need, how they're doing. You learn and grow with the plants. You belong. By missing this, we deny ourselves so much enrichment. It is undoubtedly scary taking on an allotment for the first time, as it is any first-time gardening enterprise, but I firmly believe that if I can do it, anyone can. And the evidence of June is that I can.

On 1 June, Gill, an old journalism friend, drives for an hour to visit. She's heard about the allotment and wants not only to see it, but to help. We pull up weeds, pot up kale and Roman-esco seedlings, pot on aubergines and rudbeckia and plant more rudbeckia out in the herbaceous border. They look so fragile outside. I can only hope that they'll survive. But it's June and we are absolutely past the last frosts now, so they should. By August they will be sturdy plants, bearing their distinctive yellow-brown daisy-like flowers that sway in the breeze, attract the bees, and go on metaphorically smiling until the first frosts.

After we've planted the rudbeckia, Gill and I harvest the garlic. Prior to this, I'd only ever bought garlic bulbs from either the supermarket or the farmers' market, so this is a magical moment. All the way through this year a common thread of the conversation between those of us who are new to this (Geordie,

Barbara, Garry and Kasia) is, 'It's amazing. It actually looks like the ones that you buy in the shops.'

This is true of the garlic. In November, I'd put a couple of rows of garlic cloves in the small amount of soil that was available, and hoped. Now, bunches of garlic are drying in the shed. It looks edible. It is edible. It wasn't difficult. In fact, it was easy. The supermarkets' grip on me is lessening. If I can grow garlic, then it is entirely possible that the beans, tomatoes, squash and purple sprouting broccoli will all grow too. If they do, then I will seldom have to buy imported vegetables in a supermarket. I am free.

At the end of the day, I gather all the tomato plants that my immediate allotment neighbours don't want and take them home in a large cardboard box. I walk door-to-door like a travelling salesman, asking if people want free plants. They do. After ten minutes all the plants have new homes and the notion of growing your own is seeping into the ordered gardens of the street.

The vision of what's possible expands with the lengthening days and the growing plants. Not knowing what I was doing, I haven't grown enough garlic for the year. But next year, I could rectify that and grow enough for 12 months. I lean on my spade and glance over the fence at Dan's plot. He's a hard-working young chef, with a girlfriend: surely enough to keep any man occupied, and certainly prevent him from growing his own food? Last year his presence was intermittent but enthusiastic. Really, I don't know how he found the time at all. It was impressive, working split shifts in a busy kitchen. This year, he tells me, 'I won't be there so much.' The consequence of this is that his plot has become a meadow. Mallow, poppies, verbascum all abound. It's beautiful. It's giving the soil a rest. But equally, it's driving me mad. Creeping buttercup, couch grass and, worse, Boris Johnson weed, are creeping down from his plot into mine. I thought I'd rid my plot of them, but they're back, happy to grow in the freshly tilled, enriched soil. Just think what could be grown on there, I muse. My name is down on the list for the day when Dan faces his own reality and gives up the plot for activities more associated with a chef in his twenties, whether or not he stays in the UK or returns to Canada.

The vision of the future on Dan's plot will have to wait, as the present has to be kept up with. Commuting, developing the Chelsea Flower Show project, taking care of a mother in her nineties, keeping up my love of horse riding, going to church, seeing friends, would be enough. June means that the part-time job at the allotment has reached its peak: I'm putting in 17.5 hours a week to keep it fed, watered and to begin to shape it for its first year. There is little time for sleep, and despite being surrounded by the prospect of food, there's little time to eat, either.

So perhaps it's no wonder that, by mid-June, I'm the worse for wear. A raging sore throat becomes a cold. I nurse myself quietly for three days. One more day would see it vanish. Instead, work commitments require me to hop on a train and head for Liverpool and three days' reporting, as some of the old journalistic life still exists. I top this off with a day's filming on a sheep farm, where we're explaining the meaning of Psalm 23, sheep, shepherd and all. It's rather fabulous. My job here is unglamorous: ensure everyone is fed, watered and happy, and that at the end of the day we have all the stills and footage that we need. However, it's not an ideal day for filming: windy, wet and chilly. I'm rigged out in my thickest winter jumper, a scarf, winter coat, gloves and woolly hat in June. The farmer brings us cups of tea to take the chill off. By the end of the day, I can barely stand with exhaustion and have a cough that bends me double.

Time passes. The cough doesn't shift, having well and truly moved in. I stay at home and wait for it to depart. By 4.30 p.m. one day, I can bear the four walls no longer, and drive (unsafely) to the allotment, simply for the fresh air. The salmon-pink rose planted at the entrance is in bloom. Bees feed on the salvias. I pull up fresh stretches of Boris Johnson weed. Then, suddenly, that's enough. The tomato plants need to be tied to their bamboo canes to stop them flopping over and breaking. It's too much. The greenhouse is full of plants desperate to get outside. That's too much as well. I pick a basketful of sorrel, spinach and the Japanese salad leaf mizuna, strawberries, rhubarb and broad beans and head, unsteadily, for home, uplifted by the fresh air and the fact that, whatever is happening to me, life goes on here.

Slowly the cough abates. But it's had a nice time in my lungs and is reluctant to leave. However, as midsummer approaches, a flower festival is held at my mother's church in a nearby village. Having grown up in a village, attending not only church but its fêtes, bring-and-buy sales and harvest auctions, we are programmed to attend.

My mother is rather like a rudbeckia: bright, sunny, cheerful and long-lasting. At 91, however, her petals are starting to fade; her memory too. Her spine and legs are riddled with arthritis, so walking has become difficult. However, anything that involves people and a trip down memory lane is A Good Thing. So I scoop her up and we head to her church. The village gardeners all give their extra plants for this annual occasion, some growing specifically for it. You can buy anything from a tree for a couple of pounds to vegetable and herbaceous perennials for just a few pence. I buy a tiny pot of perpetual spinach for 50p, knowing that this will give me leafy greens for months on end. What a bargain: bags of spinach leaves past their date are put on the sale shelf at our local supermarket for twice this. Yet in this little pot of potential is nearly a year's worth of spinach.

We sit in the church hall, my mother holding court, greeting everyone, somehow remembering their names, their children's names, their grandchildren's names, all of their birthdays, and eat a home-made ploughman's lunch, tea and cake. By doing so we've entered a time warp to both of our childhoods. It's reassuring, comforting, healing.

The allotment does something similar, evoking the garden that my parents and grandmother shared and the orchards around us. So being there is not just a way to feed myself, a way to reconnect with nature, it's a physical link with my past. It takes me back to the days when it was seemingly always sunny and cycling round the garden on a second-hand red bike with no brakes before breakfast was the norm; to hours, days, weeks of picking cherries; of being sent out with several large bowls and the radio, listening to Test Match Special while picking raspberries in the sun; to the earwigs that always lived in my grandmother's dahlias; growing heartily sick of runner beans; loving new potatoes and my father nurturing seedlings not only in the greenhouse, but in the adjacent cold frame.

I thought long and hard about planting cherry trees on the plot. After all, that's what I knew and loved. But I also knew that, as soon as they showed a hint of pink flesh, the beech-tree-dwelling starlings would be on them and there would be no crop for me. Tending a cherry harvest is a time-consuming thing. While I work 12-hour days, this won't be feasible. So I plumped instead for three Hampshire heritage varieties of eating apple and, as a token gesture to my childhood, a greengage tree. We had two in the garden at home. They seemed like small trees to me, because they weren't 40 feet high like the cherries. But they must have been a decent 16–20 feet. Their green fruit might look unpromising to the untrained eye, but it was delicious, juicy, sweet and invariably warm from the sun. Other than raspberries, which I could have eaten all day and night, the greengage was my favourite fruit in the garden.

The allotment greengage tree, bought from a highly reputable local grower, is looking a bit sick. It's growing, but its leaves are slightly wrinkled and mottled. The quince is also looking as if it hasn't enjoyed relocating to the plot. Under Fran's instruction, I water them regularly and hope that, in the fullness of time, they will settle, grow into strong healthy trees and produce wonderful yields of fruit. When I eat the first greengage from this tree, I know I'll be transported back to my childhood. It will be far, far more than eating a green plum.

Long summer days mean that there is now time to return home from work, eat, restore a semblance of balance to my mind and body and then head over to the allotment to look after the plants. The quick dash through on my way home, drooping with hunger and tiredness, turned out in entirely inappropriate work clothes, is now a thing of the past.

The allotment is the place to be in the evening. My lovely cottage garden faces east and is perfect for a cup of coffee in the morning, a spot of lunch or even a cuppa in the afternoon.

But by the evening, the sun has travelled over the roof and the garden is in shade. I'm a big fan of shade. It adds interest to a garden. But if I want an evening quietly spent away from people, phones and the demands of life, the south-facing allotment is the venue. It's a pleasure to watch the sky change colour over the long horizon: blue, then violet and pink; then every shade of orange and red as the sun dips unglamorously behind the allotment gate and the housing estate beyond.

June's longer days are not always so beautiful, and for a week now it has been raining. This is misery for most people, who want nothing more than to be sipping a glass of something cool outdoors after work. For me, it's a reprieve from the hours of watering needed each week to keep the plants growing.

I sit on the floor in the shed watching the rain, working my way through packets of seeds to see what needs planting next. There is still time for a second sowing of both runner and French beans. Lettuces can be planted the year through if you're mindful which varieties you grow. And there's the possibility, perhaps, of adding one last pumpkin to the fray.

Sitting on the floor in the shed is all well and good, but having something more comfortable would be wonderful. Most allotment holders have realized this and built, or bought, a little home-from-home. Many have sofas, some televisions and computers. They often have miniature kitchens and wood-burning stoves. They are as different as the people who build them, and full of character. But I don't really need one. The floor is fine. And, unlike my peers, I don't want to stay all day and most of the evening. I'm just here to do a job, I tell myself. The earth laughs quietly to itself.

It is de rigueur to repurpose, reuse and salvage as much as you can on an allotment. Recently, I saw someone erect an entirely new greenhouse, and it was quite bedazzling. The rest of the greenhouses and polytunnels (not to mention the sheds) are second-hand, or cobbled together from old windows and wood found in skips.

There is only one planet, even if we don't behave as if there is most of the time, so salvaging and reusing is a positive contribution. In 2016, the UK generated 222.9 million tonnes of waste, up 4 per cent on 2014. Construction and demolition generate the most, more than half in fact, at about 136 million tonnes a year. Household waste contributes a further 27.3 million tonnes. All together that's enough to fill Wembley Stadium to the roof 391 times over. There's a clue in the name: waste. Surely, it needn't all be?

So in a bid to have recycling as an option, not just shopping new, I've signed up to our local Freecycle group, which over time yielded the five water butts. Geordie made me a couple of compost bins out of old pallets, and a third was constructed from a kit that my hairdresser, Guillaume, bought but never used. One morning in late June, I'm sitting in the shed doing my daily Freecycle check when I spot it: a summerhouse. It currently lives on the other side of the city in the back garden of an older couple, who are about to redesign their outdoor space after many years.

The summerhouse is six-sided. Can nothing I like be ordinarily rectangular? Its felted roof looks sound. It has two glass-panelled wooden doors painted dark grey. There are two windows to match. The rest is painted in a light grey. All the paint is peeling, and bits of wood around the base look like they need replacing. But essentially it appears unlikely to let the rain in, and certainly isn't ready to join the 222.9 million tonnes of waste going out of our doors this year. My heart sings. A summerhouse: a place to retreat from the weather, to sit on a chair rather than on the floor, to drink tea and, who knows, to store vegetables over the winter. But there is nowhere to put it. I glance over the fence at Dan's abandoned plot. It could go there.

The phone rings. It's Clare in a high state of excitement. Clare is a former national newspaper photographer. We met when we were both sent on a job by the *Daily Telegraph* in April 2007. I recall her brisk efficiency; and the fact that her car broke down. Should I stay? 'Go,' she said, 'I'll be fine.' She always was.

It struck me then that it could be useful to pitch stories to news desks with a photographer. If you have the pix already in the bag, it is much easier for a news editor to say 'yes'. Was Clare that person? The photographer with whom I used to work had moved to the States and Clare was already a very successful, known, award-winning Fleet Street snapper. What could be better? I tried pitching ideas to her for a while. They were never good enough. Then one day, about a year later, she accepted an idea, we did it – though I can't remember who for now – and the die was cast. We've worked together on and off for more than ten years.

Clare is scarily capable. She's fitted out the inside of the wide-beamed boat on which she lives, doing everything from the overall design to putting in water, drainage, ceilings and walls. When she sets her mind to something, she does it, and she does it well. She's also calm and measured. A high state of excitement is rare. 'I've got an allotment,' she squeals.

'What?'

'There are allotments opposite the mooring. Yours sounded so great, so I asked if they had any spare. They do. Just one. It's got four mature trees, so no one else wanted it because of the shade. So, it's mine. It's huge, and it's only £40 a year. I can't believe it,' she says.

I can't believe it either.

'You must come and see it and give me advice.' She hangs up. Give Clare advice? She's the capable one. Well, perhaps in this instance I might have my nose slightly ahead. It won't last.

It's a wonderful phone call because I know that this season of growth, of expansion, is about other people catching the vision of the possibility of growing their own food and, through that, the transformation that will be wrought in their lives. They'll get far more out of it than a few vegetables. Their souls will shift. My colleagues growing one or two tomato plants at home were the beginning. But Geordie is currently digging out bindweed from his plot a few yards away, and now Clare has her own plot too. It feels as if I'm passing on a torch, a special delight, the encouragement that anything is possible, that gardening is not for other people. It is for all of us. We were all made to till the soil. We all can.

I drive over to see Clare's allotment in my new role as Monty Don's junior assistant. If Clare's work is brilliant, her boat beautiful, I should have known that the allotments where she has found a space would be nothing short of heavenly. They are. No clay, junk, brambles or couch grass for her.

Clare lives on a private mooring on the Kennet and Avon Canal. You wouldn't know you were five minutes' walk from the town centre. Her boat is like living in a bird hide. Ducks peck at the hull, tame swans visit her daily asking for food, geese raise their goslings next to the boat.

There is no time to drink this in over a cuppa, she says; we must go straight to the allotment. So we head off across the lawn, over the Monkey Bridge and into the terraced back streets of the town. Five minutes' walk from Clare's boat are walled allotments, kept neat, tidy and ordered by all their members. It is a far cry from the higgledy-piggledyness of Winchester.

She leads me to the plot. A shed is set against the wall. The trees undoubtedly cast shade. But they have a wonderful story behind them, which makes them a blessing, not a curse. In 1996, some 10,000 mature trees were bulldozed to create the Newbury bypass. In the pause between this wanton destruction and the building of the road itself, thousands of long-dormant acorns, and other seeds, took the opportunity to grow, and the whole area was green with little saplings. These too would have ended up under the tarmac, had it not been for the vision of Phil Pritchard. He led others in potting up the seedlings and rehoming them around the country. He planted three little oak saplings and a silver birch sapling on his allotment. Clare has now taken it on. Not only can she grow vegetables, fruit and flowers, she is the custodian of these special trees, known as RefuTrees, descendants of mature trees felled in our desire to travel across the country faster. They are poignant and special. Clare is profoundly moved by them.

There are plenty of vegetables that will enjoy growing in the shade of the RefuTrees, including perpetual spinach, one of Clare's favourites. And beyond the shade, there is masses of sun-filled space. Clare explains what she's going to do. I half-listen and run my hands through the soil. It is black, friable loam. Put a pencil in here and it would grow into a tree. Everything will grow.

'You have no idea how lucky you are,' I say.

'Oh, I think I do,' she says, 'and I want to get started now.'

June is not a good time to travel if you have an allotment. Everything is growing and needs regular care, attention and water. But before the month's end, I'm heading off to the Yorkshire Dales with producer James and cameraman Scot. We're filming the story of a man for whom Psalm 23 is very important. A keen caver, he used to recite it before every expedition, though he didn't have a personal faith. On one particular day, the cave flooded, killing another caver. He could see no reason why his life had been spared, and the words of the psalm drew him to a profound, life-changing faith. His is a story that will be told as part of the Psalm 23 Garden media output. We're filming now because it's finally sunny and so the little video will look beautiful.

The three of us foregather in a service station car park and head up to Yorkshire in one car. There is plenty of time to chat. We talk of everything from motorbikes to children, work to holidays. There's a lull. I mention the summerhouse. What's their opinion? 'Get it,' they say in unison. I send the owner a message, confident in the knowledge that the summerhouse will already have found a new home. Nothing lasts for long on Freecycle.

The next day, in a break in filming, I check my emails. The summerhouse is available. I can have it. The possibilities of a comfortable future are opening up before me. 'Better check it's sound,' says James. So I ask a handyman from home if he'd be willing to check it out for me. He's a carpenter first and foremost, so knows what he's looking at. He rings back. The roof and floor are sound. The base of the walls and doors need replacing because they're so weathered, but that's easily done. Then, it is crying out for some paint.

I'm sitting on a granite rock overlooking a long valley with one farmhouse in the distance. Everything else is big wildness, God's own country. The sun is at my back. The allotment barely seems real. The summerhouse less so. 'Let's get it,' I say.

The three-day trip to Yorkshire goes well. The filming and photography are beautiful. James coaxes the right words and actions out of the former caver. It will undoubtedly be a very moving story. The weather holds. No one falls in the cave and hurts themselves. It's an unqualified success.

Back home, I'm facing up to the reality of finding a home for the summerhouse. I may have designs on Dan's plot, but it's still his. It may be for years. So where is the summerhouse to go in the meantime? Jason, a middle-aged, dark-haired man, has a garage on the allotments where he keeps a tractor. It's the strongest thing around and has a big area of grass next to it. 'Would it be possible,' I ask him, 'to put the dismantled summerhouse up against the garage, just for a bit?' 'It would,' he says and walks off.

My allotment neighbours Merv and Jim, and Alan-the-handyman, volunteer to help me move the summerhouse. If we're truthful, we all know that they'll be moving it and I'll be trying to be useful. I hire a van for £30 and drive over to the other side of town. I've never driven a transit van before and it is a whole lot of fun. You can't go fast, but no one's going to mess with you. And you can see for miles. I love it.

The combined practicality of Jim, Merv and Alan gets the summerhouse down in a matter of minutes. We manhandle it into the back of the van. Then we try to add the roof. It won't fit. 'Two trips,' says Jim. So we chug back across town (with me marvelling at the fact that any of this is real), lean the walls, floor and door of the summerhouse up against Jason's garage wall and chug back for the roof. By lunchtime it's all done. The summerhouse is, if anything, looking even sadder and more sorry for itself than in the photographs I'd originally seen. But in the expanding vision of the future in my mind's eye, it has a purpose, a new life. That new life can't be seen, let alone realized, yet. But I'm confident that it will happen. I'm thrilled.

Clare laughs when I tell her about it. 'What will you start doing next?' she says. 'Take over some of his plot? It's the Occupied Territories.' I laugh too. But the honest truth is that, in my mind, I already occupy Dan's plot. Why? It's not about having more, wanting something bigger and better. It's about looking at untapped potential and thinking, 'Wouldn't it be wonderful if that potential could be realized? Now, what can I do to make that happen?'

I won't so much be a steward of the land as a mentor of it, bringing it into its flourishing. At work, mentoring younger journalists is a real passion for me. Early on, I was employed by an editor who was, shall we say, not particularly encouraging. But at the same time as working for him, I was trained by Peter and Leni Gillman, former stellar journalists of *The Sunday Times*. I was a young nitwit who didn't know which way was up, but they were encouraging, directing and offered hope. The fact that I spent more than 30 years scribbling for a living is entirely down to their investment in me, which was unearned and unmerited.

It's been good to pass that on down the years, to see people who have little confidence in themselves or their abilities grow, flourish and never look back. Often they've been young women, still so easily overlooked in twenty-first-century Britain. I choose wisely, and have always been rewarded by watching wonderful careers; people reaching, if not exceeding their full potential. Now it is time to do this with the allotment. Dan's plot could just be my next mentee.

JULY

Abundance

The plot is now unrecognizable. Various types of bean plants entwine themselves up bamboo wigwams. Tomato plants are now 2–3 feet tall. There are sufficient rows of lettuce to feature in Mr McGregor's garden. The serried ranks of inherited raspberry canes that Geordie and I moved to their current spot in front of the apple trees last year are now standing tall and proud, in full leaf. At their feet, the few strawberry plants donated by Fran from her garden have gone wild, spreading everywhere, and yielding delicious fruit.

The tiny pot of perpetual spinach has burgeoned and is living up to expectations and giving me a daily yield of leaves. Rhubarb, cucumbers, lettuce, sorrel, beans and peas all come home with me on a nightly basis. Where there was nothing, there is now abundance.

The first day of the month is sunny, bright, blue-skied with scudding clouds. It can't be spent at the allotment. James, Scot and I have a day's filming to do at a beautiful private house and garden in Wiltshire. James has chosen the location as the setting for two important films for the Psalm 23 Garden. In the first, my boss, another Rachel, will explain why we're doing this. In the second, our colleague, Luke, will explain how the imagery of gardens runs through the Bible. Rachel is a former TV journalist. Luke is an actor and preacher. Both are superb in front of the camera. James and Scot are also brilliant. There is nothing to worry about. So my tasks extend to the usual round of ensuring everyone's happy and providing food and drink.

We park, as bidden, where the public does and walk down to the house, gravel crunching underfoot, peacocks calling nearby. We are all on our best behaviour. We are so grateful to be here, we say. We'll stay out of the way. Thank you so very much. Please do accept these flowers (coals to Newcastle) as a sign of our gratitude. And so on. The lady of the house shows us around, particularly to the places that we might work without making a nuisance of ourselves. We pile up our mounds of kit and get on with it.

Psalm 23 is highly visual, with its 'green pastures' and 'still waters'. Sarah Eberle's design comes out of this. The aim is to encourage the creation of community gardens, nationwide, born out of this psalm. There are four elements that any such garden will need: water, meadow or naturalistic planting, a tree and somewhere to sit to enjoy it all. James has chosen the location because the gardens incorporate all these elements, subtly, without needing to be stated.

Clear, chalk streams run through areas of mighty trees. An old wooden bench in the lee of a wall is covered in lichen and surrounded by exquisitely scented roses. And there are areas that have been allowed to turn into wildflower meadows, full of native grasses, clover, buttercups and orchids. It is an embodiment of the psalm.

Luke goes first, walking through sunlit borders, sitting on the bench, standing on a bridge, knowing his lines, speaking with assurance and passion. Then comes Rachel, whose job it is to stand by one of the streams, and talk. She knows what she's doing and the whole thing is expertly completed in just a few hours. Then it's time for a bit more filming and some stills photography. I sit in the sunshine with the pile of kit and write the pieces that will accompany this. Then I fall sound asleep and wake up with sunburn.

Back at the allotment the next day, now wearing suntan lotion in a stable-door-bolting-horse fashion, it's time to dig the onions. I planted a couple of rows (27 onion sets) last November, expecting little. Yet here they are, a mix of red and white onions, ready to be harvested. I dig my fork underneath them and shift the earth slightly to avoid damaging them. Out they come, one after another, pungent, colourful, glistening in the sun.

It's important to leave onions out in the sun to dry off before putting them away for the winter. The stems are still green. And this growth needs to die back completely so that the onions can be stored successfully. I cobble together a low structure made out of wood and topped with chicken wire. The 27 onions lie on it to dry off. Around the allotments, people are harvesting hundreds of onions. So 27 doesn't seem like very much. But it's 27 more than I've ever grown before, so it's a success. It is abundance. Just like the garlic, now I know it's possible, I can grow more in the future. I gain a little confidence in the second year and grow a few more, but still not enough. A few days ago, now planning for my third season, I've planted 120 onion sets and 66 garlic cloves. There's space for a few more. Who knew that such abundance could come from such a small space? As a small person (I'm 5 feet 2 inches, and currently my godchildren, aged 9 and 11, are about to exceed me in height), I find this very encouraging. When you're small, your whole life is about being overlooked. If even children are taller than me, then adults certainly are. I'm physically looked down upon. That has led to some notable instances of being looked down upon in attitude too. At the start of my career, being young, blonde, female, inexperienced and small meant I was also insignificant. Now that I'm middle-aged, instead it means I'm invisible. It often felt like the only tactic open to me was to be feisty, rather in the manner of a small pony. I was keen to always exceed people's expectations. But proving yourself continuously for more than 30 years is a pretty tiring affair, especially in workplaces that have an unconscious male bias.

The onions haven't had to be forced. They simply grew. The allotment is abundant. If that's true for a small space, can it also be true for me? Can I be abundant without all this effort? Perhaps I already am. The onions are onions; perhaps being me is enough, whatever might have been inferred to the contrary. That's rather a restful thought.

Every evening, after I've watered, I gather food for my evening meal. Cucumbers, broad beans, lettuce and mizuna are the regulars, and until the middle of July I can still harvest rhubarb. After that, it needs time to rest and regrow ahead of its winter die-back. Stopping eating it soon means I'm assured of more rhubarb next year. There's a small message in there: you can't simply take. You have to give back. Everything needs rest and recuperation in order to go forward into the future.

How difficult that is to live out in practice. The tyranny of the urgent, the next thing, the diary, the things we ought to do, the people we must see, can mean that life is relentless. There is seldom time for rest and recuperation. And we wonder why we're so exhausted and burnt out. If I need to copy the onions and be myself, then I also need to learn from the rhubarb and refrain from going at all of life full-tilt.

This week, the daily meditations I listen to have been all about how Jesus took himself off quietly in order to recharge his batteries with God. FOMO (fear of missing out) can stop us doing this. Surely there's something more interesting to do, watch, listen to? But if it was a basic necessity for the Son of God, then stopping is needful for us too. I am very, very bad at this, but again, the allotment offers opportunities to change course. If I sit for long enough gazing at the plot, my mind quietens, and in the quiet there is the chance for God's presence to be known.

But this is not always the case. As it's July, there isn't much sitting down to be done. It's all watering and harvesting. Because of the Mr McGregor-like lettuce harvest, there are plenty of salads on the menu, including one with broad beans, onions and bacon. Rhubarb crumble, rhubarb cake and rhubarb gin take over the kitchen.

Meals are based on what I have. I no longer think what I'd like to eat and then buy the ingredients. It is a small but, equally, dramatic shift in thinking. According to a BBC poll in 2014, we have lost our understanding of the seasonality of British food. Step into your local supermarket on any day of the year and you can buy strawberries and oranges, apples and asparagus, lettuce and tomatoes. It's easy to see why many of us don't have a clue about when these fruit and vegetables are in season here in the UK.

Of the 2,000 people polled, only 5 per cent knew when to pick blackberries (July to mid-September), 4 per cent knew when plums were at their juiciest (August and September) and one in ten knew when to head to their local pick-your-own for gooseberries (June and July). This is despite the fact that 86 per cent of us say that seasonal eating is important to us and 78 per cent claim that we shop seasonally.

It is easy to get stuck in the same old supermarket routine, buying a similar list of goods each week to make pretty much the same meals. In that world, seasonality doesn't get a look in.

Does any of this matter? I'd argue it absolutely does because knowing when foods are seasonal connects us to our landscape, roots us in the earth and gives us some pretty basic survival knowledge. Consider this: a glut of strawberries in June means that they will be sold at a lower price than in October. Asparagus is invariably more expensive when it first comes on to the market, but by late May or early June, the price has become more affordable. So buying in season saves you money.

Guy Watson, the founder of Riverford Organics, says, 'I am an advocate of local food, partly on environmental grounds

but mainly because I think it's important that people feel a connection with where their food comes from.' That's true. Buying
local gives you a mental map and calendar of what is grown
where and by whom. That in turn connects you to the heritage
of the place you live in. You're no longer a shopper, you're
a person rooted in a location, with a sense of belonging. The
cherry harvest coloured my childhood. The strawberry harvest
touched my young adult years, as I visited my parents (who
were by then living on the south coast) and we stopped by roadside stalls to buy freshly picked strawberries. Every area has its
own specialties. On a recent assignment with Scot, we found
ourselves in a part of the country where asparagus was sold
in roadside vehicles that would elsewhere be flogging burgers.
I was agog: asparagus sold on the roadside seemed terribly
exotic to me, but it's not if you live in an asparagus-growing
region.

Eating seasonally also means that the food you eat is fresher
and more nutritious. As we worry about increasing rates of
obesity, surely enabling more people to grow a little of their
own food has to be the way forward? This was the motivation
behind the formation of allotments in the nineteenth century.
Wouldn't it be wonderful if, rather than build more supermarkets, the land that the supermarket giants wanted was given
up for community allotments? In every town and village people
could help each other to grow food, children could get fresh air
and exercise, and the nation's health would surely improve. If I
were in charge of planning law, that would be my stipulation:
no more supermarkets; allotments instead. Allotments in poor
communities and rich, allotments for everyone, for those who
have never grown a vegetable and barely know what one is,
and for those who have regular veg-box deliveries. If land can
be compulsorily purchased for schemes such as HS2, surely
land can be bought for allotments? Perhaps this is my next job:
Minister for Allotments.

The chickpeas have flourished and are now standing 2 feet
tall, bearing green pods about half an inch long, each containing one chickpea. It's unbelievable. Now I recall seeing mounds
of the stems piled up for sale in a market in Petra, Jordan when

on a reporting assignment. I had no clue then what they were, let alone that I'd be able to grow them on this unpromising piece of Hampshire clay. But because the little plot is south-facing, a harvest will be yielded.

You can either harvest chickpeas when they're green, like this, or wait for the whole plant to die and pick them sun-dried. Phil and I think that picking them green would be a whole lot of fun. After all, what could be more entertaining than bright green hummus? So we spend a weekend learning to respect the growers of chickpeas and the makers of hummus. Harvesting the plants is simple. Chickpeas are part of the legume family, and their roots all put nitrogen back into the soil; which is to say, they feed the soil as well as take from it. So when harvesting, you cut all legumes off at the ground, leaving their roots to work their magic and then rot down.

We now have a mound of chickpea plants, and sit for hours removing the pods from the plants, telling stories, laughing, drinking tea. At the end of this, we have a garden waste bag full of chickpea plants, a heap of pods, and very green fingernails. Several more hours are spent podding each chickpea. Only then can we start the cooking process. The good news is that green chickpeas cook much more quickly than dried ones. So by the day's end, we have four plastic takeaway tubs full of luminous green hummus, which is undeniably delicious.

We also have a lot of water in which the chickpeas were cooked. This has undergone a rebranding and is now known as aquafaba and can be bought in shops. This may sound like The Emperor's New Clothes, but I kid you not. It forms the basis of vegan meringues, replacing egg whites. We give it a go. Meringues take ages. We're starting to flag. But miraculously, vegan meringues are the result. And they're more than edible.

'We must tell Geordie,' says Phil. So we head off to Geordie's house down the road, bearing lime-green hummus and vegan meringues. Geordie (who could be a professional chef) rustles up something that we can actually eat, rummages in his cellar for a bottle of white Burgundy, and the rest of the evening is a blur. Making hummus from scratch is, however, a lengthy process. The only way to enjoy it is if you share it with others.

Doing it alone is a protracted misery. I do this in the second season, because the pandemic keeps Phil and I apart at harvest time, indeed most of the time. I swear blind that I'll never grow chickpeas again. But the hummus is so delicious that I will. But what the chickpeas are teaching me is to allow time, to slow down, to work with others, and stop trying to do everything myself. Community, say the chickpeas, that's what you need. And they are right.

The sun is invariably setting as I head home from the allotment every evening. This means that I'm seldom now in my lovely garden. It's always been a home to birds, but this year my absence has allowed them more room, and they are everywhere. There's a terracotta planter on the back wall of the house by the kitchen door. It's normally full of trailing plants, like nasturtiums. This year, there hasn't been time to plant it up. So Mrs Robin has moved in, built a nest and has been sitting on the eggs for two weeks now. Normally, I'd be sitting on the patio for a morning coffee and lunch, at the very least, possibly even eating out in the evening. This year, I'm making two trips down the garden per day to feed the hens, and that's it. Mrs Robin can relax. In mid-July, I spy five dark fluffy heads with bright yellow beaks. The chicks have hatched. There's a lot of squeaking. I follow their progress daily out of the tail of my eye, pretending to Mrs Robin that I'm not looking. Rather like at the allotment, the garden has an abundance of food for the birds. Nothing is sprayed, so there are plenty of insects. Mrs Robin flies backwards and forwards, beak full, the day long. Two weeks later the nest is empty. All five robins have fledged successfully.

Back at the allotment, which I only leave to work, eat or sleep, the sweet peas are filling the air with their fragrance. The few scrappy, frost-scorched plants have not only recovered but thrived, enjoying my daily watering routine and the plentiful sunshine. They've scrambled up the fence and now they form a hedge of pink-and-purple flowers between Dan's plot and mine.

Sweet peas are the gift that keeps on giving. Pick them daily and you get more, and more. Stop picking and you get nothing, the plants go to seed and it's all over. I take a bunch of sweet peas home every day. The house is full of their delicious scent. I give bunches away. But I can't keep up. The nay-sayers (those who thought that flowers were a waste of time and that only vegetables were holy) drift over. 'Your sweet peas are doing well,' they say, standing for a longer time than you would expect by the fence. 'Would you like some?' I ask. 'Oh, well, if you're offering,' they say. I smile. I am offering. I have a super overabundance. Barbara tells me that, in Portugal, they don't have sweet peas. I pick her a bunch. She's blown away by the fragrance. 'Will you save me some seed?' I do, and the following year she has a hedge of sweet peas that stretches for at least 40 feet. Phil, though English, has somehow skipped childhood sweet-pea knowledge. He looks at them, puzzled. 'Where's the pea?' he asks. I explain: this is a flowering pea. You save the seeds to grow more, not to eat. 'There's nothing to eat? A pea without peas?' He looks simultaneously disappointed and puzzled. My mother, however, is delighted, as I turn up one evening with a bucketful of fragrant flowers.

It's as I'm picking the sweet peas that everything changes. Jim walks over and greets me in his usual fashion. 'Plot's looking good, Hazel.' He is the most encouraging of people. I stop picking and we chat. 'Laddie's giving up his plot,' he says, nodding at Dan's weed-covered plot. 'It's yours. Well, not officially. You can't have it until September. But you can start planning.' I dance a little jig. Jim smiles. 'You've done well,' he says, 'for a lady by herself', and walks off.

Other than submitting Sarah Eberle's design to the RHS for the Chelsea Flower Show, this is the most exciting thing to happen all year. The little plot is about to double in size. The possibility of more adventure, creativity and learning lies ahead. If there is abundance in the little plot, there will be overabundance in the bigger plot. This means that I can grow food with the sole intention of giving it away.

Butter mountains and wine lakes should have taught us that oversupply was Not A Good Thing, that abundance needed to be shared, not stored. It didn't seem to. Now, in the UK, people go hungry every day. In the UK, the world's sixth-largest economy. What the blazes is happening? When I was a child there was no such thing as a food bank. The Trussell Trust, a leading provider of free food to those who need it, was established in 1997. Ten years later, it was distributing 1.2 million three-day emergency food parcels to families in the UK. As I write, the coronavirus has profoundly affected this, with some 1.9 million parcels being distributed. Living in leafy Winchester, it's easy to think that this isn't a problem. But some 191,240 parcels were distributed in the South East in the last year. Winchester Basics Bank is a Christian charity that provides seven-day food parcels and clothing for those who need it. During the pandemic, the number of food parcels it gave out each week doubled to 400: that's 400 households within walking distance of my house who haven't got enough to eat. As well as those households, there will also be those who are only just getting by; those who are so busy that they seldom get the chance to buy food and thus live on thin air; and those who find it harder to get to the shops and so don't have anything fresh to eat.

Having an oversupply myself means that I can give food away cheerfully: giving away will be the purpose. This does, in fact, turn out to be the case: the summer of 2020 saw Geordie and I bringing bags and bags of vegetables back to our neighbourhood and giving them to whoever wanted or needed them. One evening sticks in my memory. Of my three cucumber plants, one was yielding more cucumbers than I could hope to cope with. I had three at home and seven were hanging on the vine. I turned to our neighbourhood WhatsApp group. Would anyone like a cucumber? Seven people replied. Mostly they were people I didn't know. I walked home over the hill bearing the cucumbers and left them on the doorsteps. Messages of gratitude flooded in. One person hadn't been able to get to the shops. Another was running low on veg. A third wanted to make a salad. For another, it was simply a nice surprise. This went on day after week after month. Right now, in July, looking at Dan's plot, knee-high in weeds, I don't know that this is going to happen. All I can see is potential, and not just the potential for myself, but the potential for others, the potential for the land.

It is now widely recognized that gardening is not just good for your physical health, but your mental health too. This may be why: gardening is made up of small, tangible tasks, and at the end (with fruits and vegetables) there's a result, a yield, a harvest. This is so different from pushing bits of paper round your desk, or a life of email and Zoom meetings, that it benefits our mental health.

Daily we can be overwhelmed with situations that we feel unable to influence: the impact of Brexit, the coronavirus, climate change, deforestation, the industrialization of farming, the pollution of rivers, the hunger of households around us. But by growing more vegetables than I need, I can help others, I can make a tangible difference. Imagine what could be achieved if, as Minister of Allotments, I put my 'no more supermarkets' strategy into practice and this became possible for millions more people. Perhaps it's a big ambition. I don't see the current government appointing a Minister for Allotments. But then, a year ago, I didn't have an allotment, and now I have nearly two, so perhaps anything is possible.

However, you should be careful what you wish for. Dan's plot is so unloved it makes mine look positively cherished. First, it's not on one level. There's a strange mound towards the top, large enough to house a greenhouse and a shed. But it's not shored up and is, therefore, in a constant state of subsidence. Second, it's a place where unwanted garden structures have come to die. There's a wonky, dark-green tin shed, standing on bricks. Next to it (sometimes) is an unglazed greenhouse. But because this has never been put on a base, it has blown away innumerable times and is now a tangled jumble of twisted metal whose door doesn't open. Third, the soil has not been nourished in the longest time. Dan planted straight into it in his first year and did amazingly well. Everything grew. But it's not had a whiff of manure, compost or any other nutrient since anyone can remember, and they can remember a long time here. Earlier in the spring, Dan had covered two areas with black weed-suppressing membrane and then burnt holes in it with a blow torch with a view to growing his plants in the holes. There are a few residual sweetcorn plants that haven't grown due to the

lack of water, and a few leeks that are holding in there somehow. Otherwise, nature has taken over. There are poppies,
mallow, horse daisies, couch grass and dandelions. And by the
fence, there's a massive clump of Jerusalem artichokes, which
grow to 6 feet high by the end of the summer. There are two
composting areas, with piles of dead stalks, and the whole thing
is overshadowed by a sycamore that grows back no matter how
many times it's cut down. It's a pretty depressing sight.

But if the little plot has taught me anything (and it's taught
me a lot), it's that a great deal can come from almost nothing.
So I'll take the 'almost nothing' being offered me and see what
it can do when allowed to flourish.

The first task is to get rid of all the Mecano-esque structures.
That's easy. Whisper it quietly that you want rid of something and someone else will want it. Four of us lift the tin shed
and take it to its new home by the gate, where it will become
a very respectable and loved store of pots. 'Think on,' says
Rose, 'you could turn that greenhouse into a brassica cage by
covering it in netting.' 'I know you're right, Rose,' I say, 'but
the door doesn't open, and I can't bear the struggle that would
be involved to fix it.' 'Alright then,' she says, and the four of
us bear it to its new home and I promptly forget all about it.

A second James (this one a graphic designer and now the
chairman of the allotments, following Jim's retirement from
the post) lends me his strimmer, and I walk round the plot cutting the weeds back to the ground. At the end, everyone howls
with laughter, because I am splattered head-to-food in green
plant juice. Sacks and sacks of weeds go to the tip for recycling.
It's now possible to see the lie of the land, and to start planning,
the only trouble being that I can't envisage what to do with it.
The potager model is stuck in my head, but it doesn't seem
to translate up here. Geordie dispenses wisdom. 'You want to
keep this open and grow all your big stuff up here, courgettes,
pumpkins, cucumbers, and then carry on with what you're
doing on the existing plot.' It doesn't seem right. It's what he'd
do. I want to do something else. It's only later that I'll realize
that he was right all along and revert to his plan. For now, I'm
spending quite a bit of time gazing and wondering.

After weeks of abundance and the promise of more abundance, the month ends with a comedy. Martin and Alison have an extensive plot next to Geordie's. Part of it is a small, well-established apple orchard that's fenced in, and it's where their hens and cockerel live. It is chicken heaven. It makes me feel rather sorry for Bandit, Ivy and Honeysuckle, living at the end of my garden, not in this kind of splendour. 'Well,' says Alison, 'why don't your hens come and live here in the summer and go home in the winter?' It seems like a wonderful offer. It is a wonderful offer. But I haven't factored my hens' nature into the equation. I'm slightly concerned about integrating the two flocks, knowing from long experience the scrapping that goes on for dominance, the establishment of a fresh pecking order. It's not pretty. Hens can be cruel. I raise this. 'Oh, we've never had a problem,' says Alison. 'It always goes really smoothly.' I want to believe that this will be the case. So, one evening, my neighbour Angela (a fellow chicken-keeper) and I gather up Bandit, Ivy and Honeysuckle, put them in a crate and drive them to the plot. The sun is setting over the orchard as we put them into the coop with Martin and Alison's chickens and cockerel.

I barely sleep that night, worrying about what's happening to my three. They are the visitors and might be at the bottom of the pecking order. And there's a cockerel. They're not used to all that that might entail. As dawn breaks, I head to the allotment, and find the hens all up, though in separate groups. My three are patrolling the fence-line, loving the deep grass, picking at grubs. Currently, there doesn't seem to be a problem.

At 4 p.m., the phone rings. It's Alison. My hens are terrorizing hers and the much-loved cockerel has died. Could I please come and collect my hens? Oh no! My worst fears are realized. Perhaps you can't name a chicken Bandit and expect good behaviour. Angela and I drive back and do the whole escapade in reverse. I really am very sorry. I offer to buy another cockerel. Alison and Martin are forgiving and kind. Not to worry, they say. He was old. It's OK. Bandit, Ivy and Honeysuckle don't seem particularly surprised to find themselves back at home. 'You naughty chickens,' I chide them. 'You've had a day out when you could have had a whole summer holiday.' And then, I sit in the hen pen and laugh.

The allotments lie on one side of the hill, my house on the other. In between, at the top of the hill, is a beautiful area of grass and trees. From 1096, it was home to St Giles Fair, the largest and most profitable fair in Europe. Now, it's the home of dog walkers. They are all very sociable. A friend of mine walks her dog up there. She meets the same people every day, including another woman with whom she had daily chats. This lady invited her to a Christmas party. Where should she deliver the invitation? My friend indicated an address near mine, on the north side of the hill. The lady blanched. The invitation was withdrawn. 'It seems,' my friend laughed when explaining this later, 'that I live on the wrong side of the hill.' And it's true: the side where the lady lived has some Very Big Houses Indeed. But our side is hardly rough. Or maybe it is. Perhaps today, Bandit, Ivy and Honeysuckle have proved that there is a 'wrong side of the hill', that we live on it, and that they have hefted to it. When offered the luxury, the abundance, of an apple orchard on the other side of the hill, they rejected it through thoroughly bad behaviour, and have returned home. Abundance has its limits.

AUGUST

The Importance of Water

If you're British, you will probably have grown up talking about the weather, specifically how wet or dry it is. Brits will greet strangers with comments about the weather – 'Dreadful rain'; 'Shocking isn't it?' – when they wouldn't normally look them in the eye. The variability of our island weather bonds us.

It bonds us on the allotment too. While we don't experience uniformly blue skies during August, we are blessed with a lot of them. And the grey ones don't yield any rain. So my job, all of our jobs, is to keep our plants alive and flourishing through daily watering.

The trick here is to give everything a good soaking, not a minimal drink. This takes two hours. Every night. I have five water butts, standing in a slightly drunken line alongside the shed. They now stand empty. So I'm reduced to using water from the standpipe. I share this with Jim and Rose, Merv and Val, Fran and Ian, and at least three other plot holders. Ours is the penultimate tap in the allotments. They all work off one water pipe. So it doesn't take a genius to figure out that, if you're towards the end of that pipe, the amount of water coming out of it will be considerably less than if you are near the gate.

Many of us can only water after work and this simply exacerbates the problem. If half a dozen, or worse, a dozen people are watering their plots in the evening, just a dribble of water will come out of our tap, and so a dribble of water will end up on the plants. I'm starting to have an inkling of the seriousness of water poverty. At home, I can turn on a tap without a thought (perhaps there's a problem there), but around the world, one in eight people do not have access to clean, safe drinking water, let alone water to help grow their crops. Think about that for a moment. One in eight people. Imagine if one in eight people that you knew didn't have clean drinking water. Imagine if you didn't, or I didn't. We'd be up in arms, wouldn't we? Yet, somehow, access to water is invisible. It's an invisible benefit for those of us who have it. It's rather like breathing the air: you simply consider it as natural and normal. If you don't have it, your problem is invisible too, though much commendable work is done by charities trying to change the situation.

It's only when water doesn't come out of my hosepipe that I start to consider that this must be a daily reality for many people around the world. I mutter, darkly, about the absence of a good water supply all the time. But why do I think there should be one? Access to water isn't a given in life. I just happen to have been fortunate enough to have had a ready supply of clean water all my life, and it's rather skewed my outlook.

Geordie's solution to the water problem is to be the early bird. He arrives at the allotments, having dropped his children off at school, around 8.30 a.m. Only a few keen individuals are there then, so his enormous plot is easily watered and looks, as a result, Instagram-able. On commuting days, I'm up at 6 a.m. for a 7.15 a.m. departure. Getting up at 5 a.m. to water the plot before work feels like a grinding impossibility. On non-commuting days, I'm unwilling to set a 6 a.m. alarm. You get out what you put in, and as I refuse to go early (when there's water), I have to put up with going late (when there's not).

Why does this matter? Because, without water, these plants are simply going to give up and die, meaning there's no food at the end of all this hard work. This is the peak growing season. Everything is in full song. So if I want food, daily hours of watering are what goes into it.

How much to water? Geordie and I agree that we count in our heads and when plants have had a certain amount, a certain number, we move on to the next one, and so on. Where to water? Water the base of the plant, get as close to the roots as you can, and the water will be absorbed. Water dripping down leaves may look lovely, but it's not much use to the plant, which can't absorb water through its leaves.

So, most evenings, as the sky changes colour from blue, to lilac, to pink, to gold, I stand, counting, first by the tomatoes, then the lettuce, then the beans and so on. Once a week, each new tree gets a bucketful of water with some plant feed in it. The trees will need water whenever it's dry for the first couple of years.

All this leaves me Really Rather Tired. My boss expresses the opinion that it sounds like far too much hard work. It is. But it's the reality of growing food and thus of eating and staying alive. A quick whizz round the supermarket, or ordering an online delivery, leaves you with no idea as to how much effort went into nurturing, growing, feeding, watering and protecting your food. It's hard to appreciate your meals fully. Everything I eat, I've worked hard to grow, and so I revel in whatever is on the plate, whether that be broad beans, lettuces or patty pans, which are responding so well to a daily watering routine that I'm taking several home every night and can't keep up with them.

If digging was meditative in January, watering is meditative now. There's nothing to be done except care for the plants, pay attention to what I'm doing and let thoughts drift in and out of my mind. Stillness comes after a couple of hours and the raging torrent of thoughts, problems, arguments and questions of the day pours itself away into the soil. So this is both good for the plants and good for me.

Some plants need more watering than others. The sweet peas, majestic in their purple-pink-and-lilac blooms, are continually threatening to go to seed if sufficient water isn't supplied. It feels impossible to supply as much as they need, and by the end of the month, the show is over, seed heads abound, and the air is no longer full of the heavenly scent of sweet peas. This wouldn't happen to Monty Don, who would probably still be picking sweet peas in October.

Neighbours now nip off a few seed heads when chatting, rather than picking a bunch of flowers. This gives me an idea. I can harvest the seeds and give them away to friends and relations. Gardens across the country could be filled with these delightful blooms, and with the intoxicating scent. I fill a large cooking bowl with drying pods and dream of their futures in London, the Cotswolds and the Home Counties. It is a wonderful image and allows me to continue to give things away when I thought that everything was finished.

The squashes, tromboncino and pumpkins all need plenty of water too. Fran has introduced me to a simple slow-watering technique. By each plant, I've dug a terracotta pot into the ground, placing a pebble over the hole in the bottom to slow the water flow. Each day, I fill the pot up with water, several times, and it slowly flows to the roots of the plant.

Despite this, my evening arrival is often greeted by limp, drooping leaves on the squashes, who have to be rescued, watered and rewatered before they take their natural shape again.

Tomatoes too will tell you when you've got it wrong. Cracks in the skin are testament to uneven watering: too much water one day, too little the next. Tomatoes like consistency. Anything other than that will become woefully apparent in their skins. Watering is rather like feeding. It makes you concentrate, think about the real rather than perceived need, and takes you beyond yourself.

The vegetable plants hold a mirror up to my own need for refreshment and nourishment. It is very easy to burn the candle at both ends and in the middle, to be so tired at the end of the day that there is no time to sit quietly with God and refuel the inner tank. Keep going like this and cracks appear, as they have done in the tomatoes, or you wilt, like the squashes.

It's also very easy to think that having God's presence in our lives might be a restrictive thing, limiting us with rules and regulations. But the process of watering the allotment reveals that it is the water of life, enabling us to grow and flourish. God, like water, gets into the cracks that we leave for him, and so, currently, he's seeping into my soul as I water, and calmness and quietness descend on my mind.

Over the winter, I scrounged the five water butts from allotment chums, friends and free websites. I'd thought they would be enough. I should have known that they wouldn't be. My father was committed to saving rainwater. In their extensive garden, he erected 11 water butts, taking water from shed, greenhouse and garage roofs. But one summer, this wasn't enough. There was a drought and all 11 butts ran dry. Unlike me, he wasn't about to turn on the hose. Instead, he dug a well. He reasoned that, if he dug deep enough, he'd reach the water table, and thus a well would be created and water could be drawn up for the neediest of plants.

He began digging with his garden spade. When the space became too narrow to allow him to stand inside the hole and dig, he attached a garden trowel to a long wooden pole and carried on. It must have taken days. But dogged determination won out, and he reached the water table. He built a wooden frame round the edge and attached a bucket on a long rope. Water could be drawn up each day for his most precious plants. He even made a lid for the well so that unsuspecting creatures didn't fall down it and drown.

Shortly after he'd accomplished this remarkable feat, a man from the MORI poll knocked on the door to enquire how my parents were saving water during the drought. I very much doubt that he had a box for 'dug a well'.

I used to laugh myself silly about this story. My father's endeavours made him seem eccentric at best. Now, I look back with deep respect. My solution of turning on the hosepipe is no solution at all. I should have dug a well, like he did.

Water, or the lack of it, will probably be the defining issue of the next 50 years. Climate change is bringing with it warming oceans, melting ice caps and unstable weather patterns. The UK is already being affected by rising temperatures. Between 2008 and 2017, the UK was, on average, 0.8 degrees warmer than my childhood and adolescent years. Ten of the warmest years in the UK have occurred since 1990 and nine of them have been since 2002.

At the Paris climate conference in 2015, 195 countries (including the UK) set out a plan to avoid disastrous climate change by limiting temperature rise to below 2 degrees. But as we all know, saying something is one thing, doing it another. And the world isn't on track to hit those targets. Experts believe that we may be looking at a 3-degree temperature rise, or more.

If, by some miracle, we manage to stick under 2 degrees, in the UK that will mean a 30 per cent decrease in river flows during dry periods like this August and a 5–20 per cent increase in river flow during wet periods. In practice, this is dreadful. Storms Ciara, Dennis and Jorge in early 2020 led to record rainfall levels and river levels in Wales, which saw the most widespread flooding that it had experienced since 1979. Some 3,130 homes were affected. We've all seen awful images of homes full of mud and debris, skips full of ruined household possessions, people being rescued in inflatable boats. And that's just the start of it.

In a 4-degree world, the UK government predicts 'irreversible impacts' to which we couldn't adapt. Put simply, that means higher rainfall, increased flooding and rising sea levels, as well as warmer temperatures.

In the context of all of that, five water butts feel like a drop in the ocean. But surely every drop counts? Isn't that the point? After the winter floods, Natural Resources Wales issued a report on what had happened, and it said, 'Householders and individuals also need to take a share of the responsibility.' Wherever we live, this is true. The allotment committee have been scratching their collective heads and wondering what to do about this. It is decided that water butts must be added to every structure within the allotments. We cannot afford the water that we're using, either financially or in planetary terms. So water butts are de rigueur. A delivery is made to the allotments, a lorryload of white plastic tubs that have been repurposed from their former lives as storage containers into water butts. I take three with a view to running them all off the summerhouse in the fullness of time.

Everyone else, it seems, is relaxing after work with a glass of white wine or basking in the sunshine at the weekend. They're probably not. But I am profoundly aware that this is not what I'm doing. There isn't a moment to stop. The vegetables need the sun to thrive, but I end each day smelling like a piece of cheese, through gardening in the heat. It's worth it. Every evening, I'm taking home baskets full of produce: cucumbers, spinach, strawberries, runner beans, lettuces, dwarf French beans, purple climbing beans, yellow courgettes, the first of the kale and early raspberries, tomatoes and, gloriously, corn on the cob.

Nothing can prepare you for just how delicious a homegrown sweetcorn is. The reason is simple: you can eat it fresh. With corn cobs, this makes all the difference. The natural conversion of sugar into starch really speeds up when you harvest sweet-corn. As soon as you pick one, the sugars inside it start to change, and within 24 hours, most varieties of corn convert more than half their sugar content to starch. This affects the flavour.

Pick a sweetcorn, walk home with it, boil it for 5–8 minutes, slather it with butter, salt and pepper, and it will taste sweeter than anything you've bought from the shops. I am wholly unprepared for this and utterly delighted by the result. A weekend lunch can now simply be a corn cob. Rather like porridge for breakfast, it leaves you completely satisfied. So I'm delighted to be harvesting the sweetcorn now (which really needed serious amounts of water to flourish) and am careful to take home only what I need for that day.

In fact, that is a big learning experience of harvest. Harvest what you can eat fresh at its best. After that, if you have any-thing left that must be picked today, give it away; or, if it can be preserved, do this. The courgettes, tomatoes and aubergines become vegetable stew and go into the freezer for later. More courgettes (and there are always more) become courgette cake, a hitherto unknown food of the gods. Hours are spent making chutney.

Merv and Val have several well-established apple trees on their plot. This is a bumper year for apples. They frequently leave me sacks of the windfalls to give to the horses, Marcus, Aragorn, Arthur and Ollie. But, they say, I can help myself too. There are too many. I take baskets of red-and-green eating apples home, and more vivid red cookers. Stewed apple is added to the winter store in the freezer. Marcus, Aragorn, Arthur and Ollie (and, I suspect, all their mates in neighbour-ing yards) are very happy about the apples. Aragorn (a grand, kindly bay horse) licks his lips for about five minutes after his weekly apple treat, to ensure he's got every last sweet, sugary drop into his mouth. Arthur (a small, intelligent, grey pony) stands beside him trying to catch any drop that falls.

The Swiss chard is now at the height of its powers, striking with red, yellow, white and almost purple stems and either green or reddish leaves. Like spinach, it wilts quickly once picked, so is added to the list of things to harvest and eat straightaway. All this is changing how and what I eat. Instead of buying food for a recipe, I visit the plot, pick a basketful of vegetables and work out a recipe from there.

At the allotments, we are all swapping vegetables with each other. Someone with a glut of courgettes will trade for tomatoes; potatoes are swapped for lettuces. So where you begin with superfluity, you end up with variety. 'You shall harvest what you have not sown.' How true that is, and how astonishingly humbling. As well as swapping our produce, we are swapping recipes. Apple and cinnamon loaf, courgette puff pie, brown sauce, runner bean soup, Polish pickled cucumbers and Sri Lankan runner-bean curry all get added to the cookery book and become overnight staples. A colleague gives me a book entitled *What Will I Do with All Those Courgettes?* There are more than 150 recipes for soups, salads, casseroles, bread and cake that will use up perhaps a fraction of the courgette and patty pan harvest.

My not-quite-godson and his fiancée come to visit for the weekend. They live in London, where their food arrives in a van from a supermarket. We go to the allotment. There is not much to say, as the allotment does the talking. My not-quite-godson has never seen runner beans growing before, let alone a patty pan. I hand them two bags and some secateurs and let them pick whatever they want.

Then I lead them round the allotments introducing them to friends. The friends spot that these are (thankfully) people who will readily accept vegetables. Courgettes (unsurprisingly), lettuces, tomatoes, more beans, potatoes all get added to their bags. By the end, they have enough food for a family of four for about a month. They are amazed.

They're vegetarians and I'd been worrying over what to feed them. Why was I worrying? As I am awash with runner beans, we have Sri Lankan runner-bean curry and rice. Creamy, spicy, full of flavour and, moreover, fresh, it's really rather delicious (those curious may find it on the BBC Good Food website). 'I thought that runner beans were always hard and horrible,' says the fiancée, 'but these are gorgeous.' It is a tragedy that someone should be put off runner beans because of the undeniably hard, long-picked and rather oversized runner beans available in some supermarkets. Fresh runner beans (especially when topped with a little butter, or in this case, steeped in coconut milk) are sublime. So my not-quite-godson and his fiancée have their own little encounter with the concept of fresh vegetables, and I send them home on the train, laden with carrier bags full of vegetables and fruit. In the late summer, I save some of the runner bean seeds and send them to my not-quite-godson's parents. They grow them in their east London back garden and eat runner beans for weeks on end, having sown and then planted every seed that I gave them. Perhaps there should be a book entitled, *What Will I Do with All Those Runner Beans?*

Fran and Ian have five chest freezers, which come into their own at this time of year. They can freeze fruit and vegetables quickly and worry about turning them into meals much, much later. I have two small freezers: the equivalent of one grown-up freezer. By now they are bursting at the seams with passata, plum tomatoes, more runner beans (in fact every sort of bean), hummus, plums, stewed rhubarb and apple, and every kind of vegetable soup.

I've made more chutney than I will ever eat or give away. So now I need some other form of preserving fruit and vegetables. After insufficient consideration of my options, I buy a hydrator. If I'm honest, this isn't a great purchase, simply because it takes so very long for anything to dry out: days, not hours. Leaving it plugged in, slowly drying apple rings, seems a bit unsafe as I head off to work, so it's only ever deployed at the weekends, rather missing the point of this keeping-up-with-the-harvest lark. But it has its place and, as the weeks go by, jar after jar of dried apple rings are added to the store cupboard.

Elderberries hang thickly over the gate to the allotments. I stand back and wait for someone else to take them, but nobody does, so I pick a few pounds and make elderberry cordial. Home-made elderflower cordial is the taste of early summer for me: sweet, fragrant, floral and refreshing. Rather like the sweetcorn, it's a different creature from its shop-bought cousins. Home-made elderberry cordial, it turns out, is a serious, grown-up sort of a drink, something that looks like Ribena but tastes as if you should be drinking it standing up, paying attention. Later, I'm emailed by a health firm called Sambuca, offering me the health benefits of what it refers to as 'black elderberry'. I know that this simply means the vitamins drawn from elderberries, and am ahead of the game with bottles of elderberry cordial. I'm not the customer.

The little pear tree is yielding pound after pound of pears. They are crisp, firm but juicy. And the Victoria plum tree is having a quiet year, but there are still more than enough plums to eat, preserve and give away.

It's a joy, but it's relentless. It slowly dawns on me why this is. At harvest time, your job is to harvest. My grandparents' generation stopped everything (school and work) for six to eight weeks over the summer to ensure all the harvest was brought in at its best, then cooked up and preserved for the coming winter months. Trying to harvest while commuting to work is the very edge of madness. Trying to achieve a sustainable life is, at the moment, unsustainable. It's not just me. All the allotment holders who go to work are, by this stage, looking drawn and tired. 'Are you keeping up?' is the endless question. 'Of course not,' is the general reply. Only those who no longer work look calm and on top of the situation.

What's to be done about this? We're not all suddenly going to revert to being subsistence farmers, at least I hope not. Imagine what would have become of the economy if that were to be the case. But things do feel out of kilter. As I write this, I've spent six months working from home, grounded by the pandemic. While I still struggled to keep up with this year's harvest, it was a little bit more achievable. Take three hours out of the day and spend it in a car on a motorway, and even the long summer days won't be enough to harvest and process your food properly. But as I write, those three hours have been different. I've been able to join Geordie in the before-work watering gang, leaving the after-work hours for harvesting and cooking. There are still never enough hours in the day. There certainly isn't enough water in the tap. A dry spring followed by a dry summer might have been lovely, but was tough on my vegetables, which didn't flourish as well. But without the commute, at least attempting to water and harvest felt more achievable, more human, fractionally less relentless.

Perhaps the lesson from this is that we are meant to live in harmony with our surroundings, with the seasons, with what's growing, not fight against it or try to shoehorn it into tiny fragments of our days. As we allow ourselves to do this, a natural rhythm of life is achieved. We are not meant to be consumers. We are just one more species on the planet. Perhaps it's time to reset the dial. Or perhaps there will always be too much to do.

Finally, on the last day of the month, I head to the allotment, clad in my habitual summer dress, to water everything, and the weather beats me to it. The sky darkens. Heavy clouds roll over the hillside. The wind gets up. I abandon the bunch of late summer flowers that I've picked and a trug full of vegetables, as suddenly the heavens open and heavy rain falls. With it comes relief for the soil, the plants and for me. I sit on the dusty floor in the shed, gazing out of the open door, as the wind whips the branches of the Victoria plum tree, blows Rose's dahlias right and left, and causes my pink cosmos to bob about over the path. This is helpful rain that falls steadily, over hours, not minutes, and gets right down to the roots of all the thirsty plants. It is, without doubt, the loveliest thing I've seen all month. And it's not often you'll find an English person saying that about rain.

SEPTEMBER

Thankfulness

The heavy rain on the last day of August, added to the month of sunshine, has turbocharged the vegetables. Refreshed and revitalized, everything continues to grow and put forth fruit. The tomato plants are draped in tomatoes, which are colouring up nicely. Both the runner and purple climbing beans have grown so rampantly over their bamboo wigwam supports that they are too heavy for them and lean at rakish angles. The purple sprouting broccoli has filled its cage and looks as if it could go on growing easily, if only there were more room. And the potatoes, which I planted specifically for my mother and Phil, have recovered from their spring frost scorching and are about 3 feet high. Soon it will be time to dig them up and see what magic lies beneath. There are rows of luxuriant lettuces, and the tithonia Red Torch, once little scrappy seedlings, now stand at the back of the herbaceous border, 5 feet tall, festooned in orange daisy-like flowers, which themselves are covered in bees. All this from a few packets of seeds and some hard graft.

I lean on the fence and gaze at it all in wonder and thankfulness. I'm thankful for the yield that has come from such unpromising soil. And I'm thankful for the delicious food that

I'm eating on a daily basis. But I'm thankful for far more than that. A new world has opened up before me, and with it the idea that anything is achievable with a bit of hard work. A whole sphere of existence that I had squarely marked down as being for other people, not me, is now mine. It's interesting what can happen to you when you say 'yes' rather than 'no' and open yourself up to heretofore unimaged possibilities. The plants have, by and large, flourished. I have flourished too. I'm confident, calmer, and take the long view on things. I'm also rooted in this blessed plot. I belong here. Its evolution will be my evolution, its future mine, its flourishing and nurturing mine, its failures mine alone. This stands in marked contrast to the preceding 30 years of my life, where I was always on the go, taking every opportunity to travel to the furthest parts of the country and the world. Home was the place I came back to, but I was always glad to leave it, to have time off from its troubles and woes. Now, thanks to half an allotment plot, I'm staying still. I'm facing my demons, living with the difficult, unhappy, intractable and hard parts of life and not running away any longer. Demons? Perhaps the fear of loneliness; the worry that I wasn't achieving enough; the regular need to have a break from my dad's dementia; just the humdrum concerns of life that you can run from, but that were always there.

Having an allotment, it turns out, is about far more than growing vegetables. It's about wholeness, stability, belonging and personal growth. And, as gardening is by any stretch of the imagination an act of faith, it is also an opportunity to grow in faith, which has happened quietly and without a hymn book, or a famous preacher giving me a three-point plan for self-development. No one tells you this when they hand you the key to the gate. There is no hint that you might change as radically as the plot that you're taking on. It's not in the rules and regulations of the allotments. But it's there in the lived reality. Everyone should have this opportunity. It's a lot cheaper than therapy and involves less crying.

About this time, a Syrian family takes on the plot that once housed the goats. There are a lot of hard workers here, but the Syrians work hardest of all, often being the last to leave as the sun sets. I've spent decades interviewing refugees, hearing stories of the day that they fled, the thing that caused them to flee after years of terror, war, death, famine, whatever range of awful circumstances they faced. But I don't ask the Syrian family about this. Their allotment is their place of sanctuary, their very physical escape from the past and a place of growth for the future. They don't need questions about horror. They build a cabin out of abandoned wood and windows. Then they get growing. Their children play. The women sit and chat. I learn a few Arabic greetings (Hello; How are you? How's the plot? Nice weather), which I struggle to remember but try to deploy. I can only hope that their space is as transformational for them as mine is for me.

The Syrians are capable people, able to do whatever is needed themselves. Though my skills have developed, I'm still thankful for the abilities of others, which make seemingly impossible tasks achievable. So it is that, early in September, I take three days off work and head to the allotment for the restoration and repair of the summerhouse. I'm joined by Alan-the-handyman, who particularly enjoys carpentry, and my cousin, Laura, who has a degree in theatre design, a boat-building qualification, and can make, fix and beautify anything. They're good people to have on board.

For three days, rotten wood is replaced with new. The outside of the summerhouse is painted dark grey with contrasting pale blue on the doors, window frames and finials. I make a half-hearted attempt to paint the interior white. It doesn't go well and, a year on, it's still patchy. We clean the windows. I provide meals and tea.

While Laura and I paint and chat, Alan sets about other structural tasks. Dan's plot – now mine – had no borders. It was just a meadow of weeds that ran into the paths. Alan gives it the fencing treatment to match the original plot, which provides definition, shape and a bit of swagger.

Fran has recommended that, as the summerhouse is south-facing, an arbour be built in front of it. Once the arbour is finished, Alan swings from it to show that it will withstand the high winds that racket alongside the hillside. The opportunity afforded by a south-facing arbour means I'm leaning towards Mediterranean planting. On one corner, I hope to plant a fig tree. It's in a pot and only 18 inches high at the moment, essentially just a twig, but one day it will be tall and bear lots of delicious fruit. There's a mature fig tree in my road a mile away, so I know it can be done. On another corner I'm planning for a dessert grape. What a prospect: taking home my own grapes and figs when I'm an old lady.

They will both grow rapidly and give much-needed shade. Despite its name, the summerhouse is too hot to sit in during the summer, and just right in winter. The presence of foliage out the front will mean that it can become a summer retreat from hard work too.

The repair of the summerhouse, its charming presence, and finally the arbour, change the horrid mound at the top of Dan's former plot into something specific and intentional rather than just a mess. We're all rather exhausted, but the plot is undergoing a transformation, in only three days.

At the end of day three, my mother is set to make a royal-ish visit and bestow her blessings on the summerhouse. It's like a television home makeover programme, as we rush to paint the finials bright blue, see them dry and put them on the roof before she arrives. We are very, very pleased as she hands out compliments and praise, says that she loves the 'dear little summerhouse' and joins us for a celebratory cup of tea inside.

If this were *The Repair Shop*, there would now be a tinted shot of the summerhouse when it arrived, looking worn, tired and drear, with a rotten layer of wood around its skirts and in need of love and attention. There might even be a follow-up shot of it in a heap in pieces on Jason's plot.

Now we have the moment of transformation, and even the summerhouse itself seems thankful. It is very smart indeed (if you overlook the shabby interior decoration), has three chairs and faces south over the cricket and football pitches, and on towards St Catherine's Hill. If I were a summerhouse, I'd be glad to have ended up here.

There's an old joke about the hierarchy of British needs. It starts with a cup of tea, a biscuit and a nice sit-down; goes through a cup of tea and a biscuit, and ends up (*in extremis*) with simply a cup of tea if that's all that can be had. We are all ready for the first, sitting in or around the summerhouse, drinking tea, eating biscuits and chatting. It is then that Alan gives us a sense of perspective.

'I found this when I was putting the arbour up,' he says, uncurling his hand to reveal a thumbnail-sized white sphere that has been split in half – probably by his spade.

'What is it?' we all want to know.

'It's a sea sponge,' says Alan, 'probably about 65 million years old.'

And with that, the whole allotment disappears, and we are back in the dawn of time. In fact, we're under water. A lot of it. What land there is has been home to the dinosaurs. But they're on their way out and large mammals (bears, lions, mammoths) are ruling the day, though not here, because we're swimming with the fish. In fact, our ancestors, the hunter-gatherers, aren't going to turn up anywhere near here until about 12,000 years ago. And this little thing, that's been lying undisturbed on Dan's plot for millennia, takes us back down a vortex of time, far better than Dr Who could.

It is, however, very hard to imagine that where we are was once sea. As we look out, we see the cricket and football players, the hedges of the fields that lead down to the M3, the hills beyond with their hedgerows and trees, and of course, in the foreground, the thriving vegetables and new trees of my plot. Yet the presence of the sea sponge affirms that this was once all under water. It puts the concerns of trying and failing to grow vegetables into perspective. 'Let's take the long view,' says the sea sponge. 'It's drier now. At least you can attempt agriculture.'

'I also found this,' says Alan, uncurling his other hand. This looks like a very much larger sea sponge. We're all very excited.

'No,' he says. 'It's a golf ball.'

I have no idea what either of them are doing there. But they both tell stories, as one would hope on the plot of a journalist. Both clearly remind me that I'm just passing through. My tenure here will be brief. I may be erecting what the allotment committee calls 'permanent structures', but nothing about this is permanent. The allotment and I are impermanent, and any attempt to cling to permanence, to create certainty, will be futile. It's better to accept the transience of life. After all, what will be left at the end to remind anyone that I was here? Shortly afterwards, hopefully the trees and the structures. The repaired summerhouse should last me out. But in 65 million years' time? Will there be anyone to see? This really does make me look up and beyond myself. Growing can be a bit obsessional. You want everything to thrive. But the sea sponge and the golf ball speak of a longer journey, and I am just a small part of it. What I can do, however, is to improve the soil, create habitats that will nurture wildlife, and try to leave a legacy of friendliness and kindness.

In the spirit of reusing and repurposing, the three old plastic storage containers are taken and turned into water butts to store rainwater that runs off the roof of the summerhouse. Alan uses old bricks and concrete slabs to create bases for them to stand on. I'm very smug about this, which of course, much later, will be my downfall. The soil on Dan's old plot is thick clay. Over the winter, it rains, biblically. Ultimately, the clay cannot absorb any more water. And one day, all three water butts (gloriously full of winter rain) collapse into the clay, emptying their water everywhere. I feel like the foolish man who built his house upon the sand.

But that's for another day. If we knew all our disasters ahead of time, we'd never do anything. So for now I'm cheerfully looking at the transformation of Dan's plot with the pretty summerhouse, water butts and fencing. A big space like this is, if I'm honest, rather overwhelming. I'm not much of a gardener. I don't have a grand design plan. Sarah Eberle would put her head in her hands. But by chipping away at the tasks, I'm slowly making progress, and for the top plot it is only Month One.

The top plot is now divided into four quarters: the first has the summerhouse and arbour, the other three are covered in weed-suppressing membrane while I think about what's going to happen. I should follow Geordie's advice of using this for plants that need a lot of space. He is right. But somehow I want to fiddle about with the top plot, and this becomes my downfall. I envisage four raised beds on the terrace and then match them with four more on one of the quarters. The top four are a success. The bottom four are a terrible waste of space, and a faff. But you learn by your mistakes, and what I learn is that just sitting, spending time with a piece of land and listening to it teaches you what it needs to be. You need to work with what you have and make the best of it. And in the first six months of taking on the second plot, I don't do this.

This is not irredeemable. That's one of the lovely things about gardening, or growing vegetables. You make a mistake and you can learn from it. If you don't get your garden design right first time, you can change it. You are not tied to your mistakes. They needn't shape your future. And if they do, it's because you've learned from them. That's liberating. No one is saying, 'Your mistake cost the company £50,000. You're fired.' Oddly, you grow in confidence through making mistakes. You stop catastrophizing and thinking that the world will end if you do something wrong. It doesn't. There's enough to eat. You relax and allow yourself to be human, not perfect; you become willing to learn and open to fresh ideas. You listen to the wisdom of others. No wonder it's now widely recognized that gardening is good for your mental health, as well as your physical health.

At work, the pressure is starting to mount. We're set to launch the Psalm 23 Garden at some point in November, though we don't know quite when, as we will follow the Royal Horticultural Society's launch, and their date isn't set yet. So

I've issued a decree that everything (website, videos, social media, photography, press releases) should be ready for the end of October, in case a starting gun is fired on 1 November. This is now focusing a lot of minds and leading to the usual last-minute scrabbling about. Videos need polishing and subtitling. Press lists need firming up. Most days are high speed, with long to-do lists and everything taking longer than you think it will.

But at the plot, there is the balance of the natural speed of life. Lettuces grow at their own rate. The potatoes become ready to harvest when they've had enough time in the soil. The tomatoes ripen when there's been sufficient sunshine and warmth for them to do so. And the courgettes, now fully into their stride, just keep on giving.

The days are balmy and still, but noticeably shorter than the height of summer, when you could leave the plot at 9 p.m. and get home in the light. There is little time after work to do anything, even water. I skid through the gates at 6.30 p.m., after a day of deadlines, but the sun is setting by 7 p.m., leaving an orange glow above the darkness of the city. Just the urgent cases are watered. The herbaceous border is now left to fend for itself. I walk slowly down the track, the last to leave in the glorious fading light, laden with potatoes, beans, lettuces of all description and tomatoes. At the gate, Allison has left a mushroom crate full of foot-long, glossy green courgettes. She has more than she needs and is casting these on the tide of generosity that washes around here. I'm already laden but can't walk past them, adding one to the trugs that I'm carrying, and walk home. Another courgette cake beckons. This is a refreshing change from a supermarket delivery.

One of the distinctive sounds of our street is the reversing alarm of supermarket delivery vans. This can be at any time of day, from 6.30 a.m. until 10 p.m. We're a mixed bunch, so the full range deliver here, from Tesco to Waitrose, as well as the organic veg-box people and the milkman. I'm more than a bit of an outlier as I walk home, laden with vegetables. This is now so normal for me that I don't even notice what's in the trugs. As I walk home, a young woman runs past and then leans panting against her house. 'Good run?' I ask. She smiles and we chat. 'Those are amazing vegetables,' she says. 'Where did you get them?' Not in a supermarket delivery, that's for sure. I explain about the allotment. 'Oh, you're Hazel,' she says, the fame of the plot having gone before me on the street's WhatsApp group, as Geordie and I dish out extra vegetables to unknown neighbours. 'Wow, they're amazing.'

Then we fall into conversation about vegetables. She's trying to grow some in her back garden. Some things have gone well, others not. This, I reassure her, is quite normal. It's not failure. She can learn from both successes and failures. 'Really?' 'Yes, really.' 'I'm fed up with my broccoli,' she says. 'It's not flowering at all.' 'Well, it won't,' I say. 'Wait until next March and you'll be eating broccoli for breakfast, lunch and tea. For now, cover it in netting and let it get on with itself.' She breathes a sigh of relief. 'Oh, I thought I'd done something wrong. I was about to rip it up.' I reassure her that this is the natural course of things with broccoli, that waiting is the right thing to do; and somewhere in the background, I can hear the broccoli breathe a sigh of relief too, knowing that it's being given the chance to flourish and come to its maturity.

In our fast-paced, deadline-driven world, with crammed diaries and never a minute to let up, we just about have the patience to allow a radish to grow or a lettuce, but purple sprouting broccoli can make us tear our hair out. The lesson from all of this is that things take their own time, and we should let them. We are the ones with the faulty timescale. Once you start to become attuned to the growing seasons, you can have the patience for broccoli, and therefore the patience for a lot of other things that take longer than you'd like. You take the long view, not the short. And that's something to be thankful for.

However, this doesn't mean that I walk into the office and say, 'Don't worry chaps. Forget the deadline. Get it done in your own time.' That would be both daft and unprofessional. But it does make me notice that, like the plants, people flourish in their own good time. Some are tall poppies, and you know right away (however young they are) that they will be brilliant. Others take longer to find their way and become themselves. Rather than feeling frustrated about that, I'm now actively thinking about how I can nurture the late developers and get them to grow. I'm mentally asking, 'What do you need in order to flourish?' rather than, 'Why don't you understand this very simple thing?' Patience – not my strong suit – is coming from growing vegetables.

As I write this, the University of Sheffield has published a report that says that having an allotment is good for you. I could have written it. Its 163 volunteers reported, 'High levels of social and community activities, including the sharing of surplus food produce, knowledge exchange, awareness and interaction with wildlife, emotional connection to their allotment, appreciation of time spent outside and aesthetic delight in the natural world.'

According to Miriam Dobson, a post-doctoral research associate and one of the report's authors, there was 'quite a wide spectrum of mental health benefits' to tending an allotment. People 'were talking about community events, the nice feeling of sharing food, knowledge and skills', as well as a 'connection to seasons and a joy in weather'.

The Guardian reports that, with loneliness a growing issue in the UK, allotments can provide a valuable community. One allotment holder said that coming together with fellow allotment holders isn't 'necessarily about connecting with people who are similar to me – it's about connecting with people you have nothing in common with apart from growing'.

In terms of physical health, Dobson notes that on top of the exercise involved in growing, people who have allotments are also 'more likely to get their five-a-day fruit and vegetables than people who don't grow their own food'.

This is what I used to call, somewhat disparagingly, a The Sky Is Blue Report in my old journalism days, a report that sets out the glaringly obvious. But perhaps it isn't glaringly obvious to others, and I applaud Dobson and her PR team for getting the news out there: allotments are good for you both mentally and physically.

This is often a subject of conversation among us. And just the other day, in the teeth of an autumn wind, James-who-fixes-everything and I stood chatting about this for some time.

We started with the mental health benefits: you see other people, you have interesting conversations, you're part of a community, you help each other, it's something to get up for, you do tangible tasks that make you feel like you've achieved something. Then we moved on to the physical benefits: you get plenty of fresh air and exercise. James and Nikki were spending several days refencing their sheep's main pasture. I was pruning, digging and planting. A day at the allotment, we both agreed, saw us doing far more than the prescribed 10,000 steps a day. James has an active job, but for me in a sedentary life, this is something to be thankful for.

There was a pause as we considered James' sheep, looked at the view and just thought about stuff. Then, finally, we said, 'And the fruit and vegetables are good too.' It was an afterthought. What you think you're here for isn't in fact the most important thing. And that's liberating when slugs eat your cabbages or pigeons eat your chickpea seeds. However much I'm keen to foster species diversity on the plot, I'm yet to love slugs and pigeons.

There's no denying that an allotment holder will have an enviable diet. A bad day is when you're only eating five portions of fruit and veg. Most days are double that. That is both a major and a subtle change, and one so literally life-enriching that I'm thankful for it on a daily basis.

On the 21st of the month, the day dawns bright and clear. It's one of those deep-blue days that you really only get in September. It's still breezy enough to be swaying the branches of all the trees, but it's mild: the kind of day that gives you a hug. The newly planted apple trees are fruiting. The herbaceous border is alive with late-summer colour: the orange of the tithonia, the purples of Fran's asters. The autumn raspberries are pumping out fruit that makes between-chore snacks. And the veg plots are singing. It is hard to believe that, just a year ago, this was junk, brambles and couch grass. With the little bit of love that I've given them, the veg plots have yielded wonderfully. It is time to harvest. First, I fill a large green trug with tomatoes, ranging from tiny yellow pear-shaped tomatoes, through to the cricket-ball-sized beef tomatoes. Next to them, I squeeze in a few aubergines and a couple of cucumbers. But that's just the hors d'oeuvre. This is followed by a galvanized bucketful of green tomatoes. There isn't enough heat in the sun now for them to ripen, and green tomato chutney is the food of the gods, so they will be put to good use. I fill a sack full of apples from Merv and Val's bounty next door for the horses. There are still a few pears remaining to be eaten, so they are added to the pile. Then there's a bag full of green vegetables, lettuces and armfuls of runner beans. Beans that have grown too big are harvested for seed for next year (and to give away). With that in mind, I fill a bag full of seed heads from the phacelia. They're dry and brown. Plenty will have seeded themselves on my plot. But these seeds can be cast on the four winds and provide patches of plants that bees will love, nationwide. It takes me three trips just to carry this to the car.

This is one day's harvest on a half plot that was a shocking mess, in poor soil, when I'm still just learning how to grow things. It is completely astonishing. Yes, I might be overwhelmed by it on occasion, but mostly, I'm thankful. And thankfulness is not something we really feel in relation to food, is it? Food is on the shelves at the supermarket. It is delivered to our door. It turns up ready-cooked from the takeaway on a Friday night. Our cupboards and freezers have plenty in them. The idea of there not being a next meal is unknown to many of us. But not to all. As I write, the Trussell Trust has announced that it is giving out six emergency food parcels every minute, here in the UK, the world's sixth-richest economy. We can't take food for granted. And, thanks to the allotment, finally, I'm not. I can truthfully say in my heart, 'For what I am about to receive, Lord, I am truly grateful.'

OCTOBER

Preserving

The spirit of thankfulness tips over into October, as we are set to celebrate harvest festival at church. The act of giving thanks for the harvest is probably innate within us, so it's done by all cultures everywhere. So while it was already a festival in the pagan calendar, it's no surprise that the Christian Church took it up, here in Britain. After all, people were already celebrating it, and the need for thankfulness hadn't changed when their faith did.

However, harvest festival always makes me rather wistful because it's changed so much. Today, we bring tins of food and toilet roll for people living in the local homeless shelter. Back then, living in a village, the rural populace brought its wares to the altar and simultaneously gave thanks and celebrated what had been grown. I was roped into helping decorate the church by my mother from early childhood. I doubt I was much help, but it was wonderful fun: gathering old man's beard and Virginia creeper to hang round door and window frames; arranging baskets of fruit and vegetables on the altar; watching the grown-ups arrange vases of flowers on every windowsill, the scent of chrysanthemums filling the air; boxes of eggs, innumerable cakes, biscuits, tarts and jars of jam; and there was always a glass of water and a piece of coal to remind us of other basic provisions.

But for me, the wondrous *pièce de résistance* was a harvest loaf baked by our near neighbour, Shirley Palmer. Standing 2 feet tall, it depicted a sheaf of corn, gathered in a stoop, with a harvest mouse climbing up it. Shirley was famed throughout the village as an excellent cook (her raspberry pavlova was legendary), but the annual appearance of her harvest loaf was one of the most exciting moments of the year for me. How did she do it? Why didn't it fall apart? It was so creative and beautiful, but I also knew from previous happy experience that it always tasted great too.

After the harvest festival service, children like me were pressed into service, filling shoeboxes with a mix of fruit, vegetables, cakes and jam. We were then sent around the village, giving the boxes to the elderly who could no longer get out and about. Everyone enjoyed that moment. Perhaps the importance of giving food away cheerfully and generously was instilled in me then.

After the giving came the eating, drinking and frivolity. A harvest supper was held in the church hall, where we ate a lot of what we'd given, and everyone had a piece of Shirley's loaf, along with some cheese. Few things were more celebrated than a piece of Shirley's loaf. It felt like an honour to receive it, and it was savoured: an interesting contrast to our modern perspective on bread.

The highlight of the evening was not the loaf however, it was the auction. Whatever goods remained were auctioned off by Ron Lacey. Ever smiling, ever capable, with slicked-back hair and a relaxed demeanour, Ron could do everything. He must have had a day job, but I was too young to know what that was. Additionally, he flew racing pigeons, kept a kitchen garden that was enormous even by village standards, had played football with my Dad, ran the youth group and buried the dead. You don't get too many Ron Laceys to the pound. He was a fine man.

He also had a mischievous twinkle in his eye, which came into its own on his big night of the year: the harvest auction. He knew just how to string people along to get the highest price for a marrow or a jar of raspberry jam. He especially knew how to get adults to bid against children, so that children like me would end up disposing of their pocket money on a chocolate cake or, memorably, a Mars Bar, for which I was comprehensively fleeced, much to everyone's amusement, except mine.

There was a lot of good-natured shouting and banter, laughing and bidding, as we sat on hard chairs, our stomachs full of good food and the ubiquitous cups of church tea. I learned at a very early age, therefore, that thanksgiving is a whole lot of fun, as well as being right and proper when you've reaped a harvest. It's good to pause for a minute, realize that you didn't achieve this unaided, turn and face God and be grateful, and then, of course, have a bit of a knees up.

Today's harvest festivals feel like lean, thin, cabbage-soup-diet affairs compared with the harvests of my childhood. It certainly helped that we all grew things, that what we grew sustained us, and that there were farmers among us too. We had a connection to the food that we brought that most don't today. But what happened to the thankfulness and celebration? Did that go with the sense of connection? If it did, that's a real worry. It is wonderfully laudable to give food to the homeless shelter, but surely there must be more to harvest than this? Surely it could be more fun?

All this was in my mind as it was announced that the church would be decorated for harvest festival at the beginning of October. A team of expert, resident flower arrangers would bedeck the twelfth-century church and it would positively glow in its autumn richness. And then there would be tins.

I decide to stage a counter-insurgency by ensuring that the church is full of vegetables too. These could then be bought by the (largely) well-heeled churchgoers, whose spirit of generosity, I figured, would enable them to be separated from bank-notes for a bag of vegetables. Plotting ensues between the vicar and me. She has a beautiful garden and grows vegetables too, so is a bit of a pushover when it comes to the vegetable rebellion. We will have an old-style harvest festival, which will surely gladden all our hearts, and the money raised will go to the homeless shelter, along with the tins and the toilet roll. Everyone's a winner.

While I may have a lot of vegetables, I don't have enough to fulfil my aim of decorating the whole church. So I pick up my trusty black wheelbarrow and walk round the allotments. It's a grey, mild, early October day and lots of people are about, picking the last of their beans, squashes, pumpkins and the first of their leeks and cabbages.

I stop at each plot, introduce myself and explain about the harvest festival. What would they like to donate? Notice, I don't ask if they would like to. There is considerable rummaging and quite a bit of fresh picking. The wheelbarrow is filled with potatoes, apples, marrows and courgettes. I add cavolo nero and patty pan. They all go in the back of the car, which has its seats down to accommodate everything. Then I go round again, like a rag and bone man. Squashes, pumpkins, onions, garlic and cabbages are all added to the wheelbarrow. The car is nearly full. James and Nikki pass me as they drive out of the allotments. 'What are you doing?' asks James. I explain. 'Oh, go and help yourself to anything from our brassica cage,' he says. 'We've got far too much.' So I add more cavolo nero, curly kale and cabbages, thank everyone, shut the car boot gingerly and drive to church.

Here, the flower arrangers are in full flow and the whole place smells of damp leaves and chrysanthemums. Most ancient churches were built in the shape of a cross. Not so ours, which is a sort of square, and runs along what was once the road to London and is now a minor back road. Just up the hill, the biggest fair in all of medieval Europe was held annually, so this was probably a busy, thriving place. Now, it's a sanctuary, a quiet backwater, a place of peace.

St John's is curiously arranged with wooden frieze, behind which are choir stalls, which are only ever used for concerts. We sit in a horseshoe shape of plastic chairs in the main body of the church, facing the altar. The presence of plastic chairs can't take away from the utter ancientness of the place, with its medieval graffiti and murals, vast wooden ceiling struts like an upturned boat, uneven stone floor and spectacular candelabra.

Now, every nook and cranny is bedecked with foliage and flowers. The vicar greets me warmly. 'Oh Hazel,' she says. 'You've brought vegetables. How wonderful', as if it's a surprise. We form a chain gang to take all the vegetables from the car to the church. Then begins the fun of arranging. Everyone else is busy with flowers, so I take up the position of my seven-year-old self and cover the altar and its surroundings with vegetables. The patty pans get pride of place on the wooden frieze. More questions are asked about them than anything else. No one has ever seen them before, yet I am awash with them. Squashes and pumpkins surround the lectern. All we need now is Shirley Palmer and a harvest loaf. But as I no longer live in the village, that's not about to happen, so this is a pretty good second best. I stand at the back of the church, leaning on one of its ancient pillars, and feel thankful. The church is in its festal finery. You can feel the very stones smiling. It is, once again, a place of celebration and thankfulness for the local harvest. The people who grew the vegetables will never see it, I reckon. But their own thankfulness for what they had grown allowed them to be sufficiently generous to give food away to some random woman with a wheelbarrow, and others will benefit from their generosity.

There are lots of 'oohs' and 'aahs' at the church's traditional state on Sunday. I'm not the only one taken back to the harvest festivals of their childhoods. But there's another surprise in store. Many of my fellow allotment holders, who donated their wares, are here, scrubbed up, clothes free of mud, to celebrate the harvest. They are treated like old friends, and encouraged into drinking cups of church tea and eating home-made biscuits. There are worse things to do on a Sunday morning. Then we have quite a prim auction, in which stupid amounts of money are given for the allotment vegetables. People really are very generous. And then they're all ridiculously pleased. Leaving church weighed down with bags of veg, they all say how delighted they are, what wonderful vegetables these are, how I'm please to thank those who grew them, and so on. So I introduce them to the allotment holders and long conversations about vegetables, harvests and growing follow. There it is. The spirit of thankfulness, which has snuck into the church with the vegetables, and is leaving with the people who bought them, though it remains hanging in the air along with the scent of chrysanthemums. That's more like it.

There's a story about a chap who had a good harvest. He was thrilled, but a bit nonplussed about what to do. So he said to himself, 'I'll tear down my barns and build bigger ones. I'll get my harvest in and then I'll eat, drink and be merry.' Unfortunately, this wasn't the right answer to the question, and God, it is said, required his life of him that very night. I've always felt rather sorry for the farmer in question. He'd had a bumper year. He didn't have to worry about where the next meal was coming from. He really could put his feet up and celebrate for a bit. Yet he dies.

Crucially, he doesn't die because of his attitude. He dies anyway. The moral of the story seems to be: you can't take it with you. This is proving to be very true at the allotments. Somehow, I'd viewed the summer months (June–September) as the time of harvest. October felt autumnal, a time of death and decay, with falling leaves and mists. How wrong I was. In October, the harvest continues unabated. It's harder to harvest, as it really is dark now after work, so I squeeze a few minutes in ahead of the commute, and fill baskets with patty pans, spinach, chard, cabbages, butternut squash, carrots and cabbage. There's curly kale, lettuce, the last of the purple climbing beans, turnips and yet more apples and pears. This goes on for days. How am I supposed to eat all of this?

The answer is that I'm not. Autumn is the time for preserving. For seven years, I ran a small preserving company. We made everything by hand from local produce and initially simply sold locally, but ended up selling to the Co-op, Fortnum & Mason and Harrods, as well as some particularly swanky restaurants. It was all a little bit mad, but it does mean that I can find my way round a preserving pan.

Preserving (making jams and chutneys) is a great way to make the harvest last. So I do. I stand for hours in the evenings, with the back door open to get rid of the smell of vinegar, cooking apple chutney, pear chutney, green tomato chutney; pureeing apples for the freezer; making pumpkin chutney and blanching the beans.

It's relentless, but necessary. Food waste feels like a crime when you've worked hard all year to raise crops. Sit down now, while I tell you some really rather shocking statistics. In 2018, food waste from UK households, the hospitality industry, food manufacture and retail and wholesale sectors, stood at around 9.5 million tonnes. That would fill Wembley Stadium to the roof more than 16 times over every year, and it all goes into the ground. Edible food. There's more: seventy per cent of that was absolutely fine to be eaten. The other 30 per cent was what's known as 'inedible parts'. Let's gloss over that.

Why worry? Well, let's look at this financially. All that annual waste has a value of more than £19 billion per year. Second, it produces more than 25 million tonnes of greenhouse gas emissions, which we can in no wise afford. Who's to blame? We all are. Me too for sure. More than 85 per cent of this wasted food comes from British households and food manufacture. We've all done it, forgotten a packet of spring onions, which languish at the back of the fridge until they become soggy; bought three packets of pasta in a 3-for-2 offer and then failed to eat the third. And so on. But really, 9.5 million tonnes of waste every year? Since I started to grow vegetables on the allotment, that means that we Britons have thrown away more than 27 million tonnes of edible food. That's filled up Wembley Stadium nearly 50 times. Get a grip.

There is a simple solution: give it away. This is beginning to happen. Supermarkets give some food to charities. But we are only chipping away at the 9.5 million tonnes. When I am Minister for Allotments, I'll persuade whichever government department is then responsible for agriculture to ban the throwing away of food. There will be food waste collections for all and a massive redistribution system that will enable food to go to those who need it. It simply won't be possible for unwanted food to remain with those who don't want it, whether they be individuals, shops, cafes and restaurants or the supermarkets. The spirit of giving away will somehow take hold.

For now, I'm looking at ways to deal with my own harvest. Preserving is one. But a great way to preserve the life of my harvest is just to give it away. This seems counterintuitive. Preserving seems to suggest keeping it for oneself for later. But taking a looser definition, it could mean keeping the food to ensure that it's eaten – by anyone. If I give it away rather than keep it for myself, I can be sure that it will be eaten and, hopefully, enjoyed. So I join Geordie on the street's WhatsApp group announcing what is on offer today: chard, spinach, cabbages, squash. People I don't know ask for what they want. I leave it on their doorsteps. It doesn't go to waste.

Rather like the chap in the story, I had thought that the fun was to be had in growing and providing for myself. It isn't. The real fun is in giving much of it away. The people in my road aren't starving, so I'm not saving lives. But some unusual homegrown veg adds a bit of interest to the menu, I suppose. I decided to grow celery in the spring, as I love it. But I've grown so much that, rather like a child in a sweet shop, I've made myself heartily sick of it, and I can't look at celery anymore, or eat any more celery soup. So I put out a WhatsApp note about celery. Yes please, say seven people. They all open their doors to find a head of celery, and I sigh with relief because not only is it not going to waste, it will be used and relished.

NOVEMBER

Renewal

At the start of November is a day so limpidly lovely that it could make you cry. The sky is royal blue and tiny white clouds scud across it. It's warm enough to take off my fleece. There's still plenty in the soil to keep me over the winter: purple sprouting broccoli, curly kale, spinach, chard, winter lettuce and yet more celery, should I feel able to face it. The last of the cheerful pink cosmos sway in the breeze on the herbaceous border, alongside the tithonia and asters. No frosts have hit us yet, but they will come, taking the flowers with them, and quite probably the lettuces.

It is a day for looking backwards and forwards. As I look backwards, I am agog that this has been possible, that anything has grown, and that I have been feeding myself and continue to do so. As I look forwards, it is in the knowledge that, if this is to happen again, if it's to go on happening and not be a fluke, then I must renew the soil. It has fed me, now I must feed it. There are multiple options: yet more well-rotted horse manure, cow manure (viewed as the king of manures:

yes, there is a hierarchy of poo), seaweed, mushroom compost or the leftovers from brewing beer. What you choose depends on your budget, your location, what you can get for free and what your soil needs. We are about to launch the Psalm 23 Garden online and in the media. Every waking moment, and many of my sleeping ones, are given over to thinking about it. It doesn't feel like I have the energy or time to return to my friend's stables and bag up horse manure. An alternative must be found.

Not too far away is a former arable farm that now grows crops to produce energy. It's a sign of our times that on a 1,050-acre estate it wasn't possible to make ends meet, as margins were cut. It's fundamentally wrong that this is the case. Now, however, the farm produces enough CO_2 to heat 8,000 homes all year round through growing biofuel crops. At the end of this process is a product called digestate. It looks like manure but doesn't have manure's thick consistency. It can be delivered in one-tonne bags. The downside is that it will cost me £50 a bag, whereas my friend's horse manure is free. The upside is that the digestate will come to me. With a tight schedule, it's an easy decision.

The limpidly lovely day would have been ideal for a mulch delivery. Instead I opt for the day after, when it pours with rain. It is biblical. I get soaked waiting for the digestate men to arrive, but they are cheerful and friendly, so it doesn't matter. Other allotment holders have jumped on board the delivery. The digestate men drop their bags off first, slowly craning them into place. I take refuge in the summerhouse and watch water stream down the windows. Finally, a couple of hours later, it's my turn. The top digestate man knocks on the summerhouse window and gives me the thumbs up. Out I go into the rain. 'Does it always rain like this here?' he asks. 'No,' I say. 'We reserve the biblical rain for guests.'

I'm starting with two tonnes of digestate, knowing that I'll need more, but somehow unable to face the prospect. (In the end, I will use five tonnes over the winter to improve my woeful soil.) The junior digestate man slowly, patiently, turns the lorry around and winches the one-tonne bags on to the top plot. I wince every now and again thinking he's going to take the new fence out, but he doesn't, having done this a thousand times before. As the second bag lands safely on the ground, the sun comes out. We are sodden and filthy. But the top digestate man looks about him and says, 'Show me round.' It turns out that he used to be a buyer for a leading veg-box delivery firm, so this is something he has said to farmers up and down the land. And now me. He's very clubbable and has that wonderful gift of making you think you're the most interesting person he's ever talked to.

I point out the curly kale, which is thriving. 'You've planted that far too close together,' he says. 'It could be a problem.' The problem, he explains, is club root. This happens when you plant brassicas (cabbages, kale, purple sprouting broccoli) too close together, or perpetually in the same spot for years, and the root forms, well, a club, rather than stretching out deep and wide. It's caused by a common fungal disease that can live in the soil for years, affecting other crops. 'If you've got it then you can't grow brassicas in this area for seven years,' says the top digestate man. Seven years? Let's be clear: we don't know that I have got club root, but now I'm sodden, filthy and worried too. There are no chemicals that will treat club root. Once you've spoiled your soil with it through ignorance or greed (or both), it's with you for enough time for you to learn from your mistake.

Despite this, overall, he likes the plot, and gives me the sales pitch on the digestate. A stick would grow in it, is the general overview, but it's too strong to be used alone. It needs mixing into soil. So long as it improves the soil, more worms flourish here and the soil's biodiversity and richness develop, I'll be happy.

In the normal course of events, who thinks about soil? Perhaps very few of us. Before all this, I certainly never did. But it might be a plan to start thinking, because we all depend on it for our food. And the news isn't good. A government survey found that almost 4 million hectares of soil in England and Wales are at risk of compaction; more than 2 million hectares of soil are at risk of erosion; intensive agriculture has caused arable soils to lose 40–60 per cent of their carbon capture; and soil degradation a decade ago was expected to cost us £1.2 billion every year. Here we have it, yet again: intensive agriculture setting the soil and the environment back, costing us the earth in every conceivable way.

The words 'intensive' and 'agriculture' simply shouldn't go together. You try squeezing more out of the soil, using chemicals, and the earth will pay you back. In desolation. (I'm mindful of this with the hint of club root, which, in the end, it turns out I don't have.) *The State of Nature* report, in 2016, said that the major decline in British wildlife over the past 50 years was linked to intensive farming practices. At this stage, one in ten British wildlife species were threatened with extinction. One in ten. With extinction. The study found that more than half (56 per cent) of British wildlife had declined. Species under threat included the turtle dove and the corn bunting.

The possibility of changing this situation has been written about beautifully by John Lewis-Stempel in his book *The Running Hare*. In this, he takes on a small field, which is surrounded by land that's intensively farmed by people he refers to as The Chemical Brothers. No wildlife lives on The Chemical Brothers' land. But through traditional, non-chemical practices, he redeems his plot of land and within a year it is full of birds, the number of worms has increased and it is home to breeding hares. It doesn't take much, or long, to allow wildlife back in.

Intensive agriculture and the system that appears to require it make me fizz with anger. It's easy to say that The Chemical Brothers are to blame. But we, as consumers, have our role to play. If we expect a loaf of bread for 50p, milk for under a pound or a supermarket chicken for a fiver, we are directly causing harm to our environment, contributing to the suffering of creatures that have a short existence before their deaths, rather than a nice life, and seeing lots of farmers go out of business every year. With that, the nature of our own environment changes.

Perhaps it's no surprise that 791 farmers committed suicide between 1981 and 1993. But we should be as outraged by this, and willing to change it, as we should about the fact that one in ten British wildlife species are threatened with extinction. We should be on the streets with placards. Failing that, however, we can shop differently: buy from small local producers and farmers, buy at the farm gate, or if that's not feasible, buy British. Ask yourself: who is paying for prices to be so low? If it's the soil, the wildlife, the chicken, the cow, the farmer, ask yourself if you could, perhaps, pay a little more to ensure that the soil is enriched, that wildlife returns, the chicken lives its full life rather than just a few months, the cow grazes outside in the summer and the farmer doesn't shoot themselves.

Through all of this, farmers like Lewis-Stempel would flourish, it would be possible for the land they worked to be continually renewed, and being a Chemical Brother would be as socially acceptable as smoking in the workplace or driving without a seatbelt.

Lewis-Stempel's beautiful book shows that small actions do make a difference. He restores a four-acre field. I can only dream of four acres. But I'm moving up from a five-rod allotment to a ten-rod one that's the size of a double tennis court, or 250 square metres in new money, and that's some kind of ambition. It doesn't really matter what size plot we all have, whether it's a window box, a patio, an urban backyard or rolling acres; we can all make a difference to the soil around us, as well as preserving it through our shopping choices.

November also marks Soil Week. Again, who knew? But as soil produces around 95 per cent of all that we eat in one way or another, it's time for me to sit up and pay attention. It wouldn't be excessive to say that we know more about the solar system than we do about soil. Yet just 1 millimetre of soil is thought to contain 50,000 species of micro-organisms. In a mere teaspoon of soil, you would find more micro-organisms than there are people on the earth. The soil beneath our feet is an incredible and yet alien world.

Rather like the rainforests (which we're also busy destroying), there is much untapped potential in the soil, much that we don't yet fully understand. How is this? Well, the micro-organisms produce antibiotics to protect them against one another. These are the basis for some of the antibiotics that we use. We are literally making medicine from the soil.

And the soil is full of wonder. Mycorrhizal fungi connect plants to each other, and trees to each other too, to the most remarkable ends. Trees and mycorrhizal fungi support each other too. Fungi give trees nutrients like nitrogen and phosphorus, and trees in their turn provide the fungi with carbon.

I may be running about with digestate, but soil takes a long, long time to create. It is thought that it takes around 100 years to build just 5 millimetres of soil, and yet it's the work of a moment to destroy soil through the use of chemicals or erosion. British soil dates to the last ice age and is 15,000 years old, which takes us back to the sea sponge on the top plot.

Soil is also a wonderful and needful storer of carbon. It stores three times as much as all the plants on earth, including trees. Intensive farming, however, releases carbon and so we are losing soil 50–100 times faster than it is being remade. If we want to prevent flooding, capture carbon, preserve our environment and, yes, feed ourselves, caring for the soil under our feet has to be at the centre of everything we do.

My friends in this endeavour at the allotment are the worms. Earthworms, Lewis-Stempel says, are like 'pistons' that aerate the soil and provide drainage. They will drag down organic matter like leaves, or in this case, the tonnes of digestate, eat it, and add to the soil's fertility. Worm casts are five times richer in nitrogen, seven times in phosphates and eleven times in potassium than the surrounding soil. So what you want is not chemicals, it's worms.

Historically, the worms on this plot have been starved, with no one adding any kind of manure in living memory. It was a heartbreaking disappointment to see how few worms there were on the bottom plot when I first took it on. Having fed them over last winter, I know there are more. They've helped feed me. So now it's my turn to put back. You cannot take without giving back in return. That is one of the fundamental lessons of this year.

But I'm intrigued to know what lies under the soil of the top plot. It's had a year lying fallow, covered in the weeds and wildflowers that Dan allowed to grow. While it drove me mad, it will undoubtedly have been beneficial for the soil, giving it a rest, with little need to give up its nutrients for the humans.

There is a biblical precedent for this. In Exodus comes the basic instruction: 'For six years you shall sow your land and gather in its yield, but the seventh year you shall let it rest and lie fallow' (Exod. 23.10–11). Why have this as a law? Because it improves soil fertility, which is what you want if you're going to carry on living. Dan's plot has had its fallow year. And, as I look about me, I realize that a fallow time needs to be incorporated throughout the plot. I now have far more space than I actually need, so I can rest an area each year and, over time, all of it will go through this natural restoration.

The act of lying the land fallow also has something funda-mental to say to all our lives, to my life. We are endlessly on the go and then wonder why we are burnt out, barely able to think, let alone function. I've worked solidly for years, hardly taking time off at the weekend, skipping holidays, inhabiting a long-hours culture. It was fun, but it was exhausting. Dan's formerly fallow plot shows that everything needs a rest in order to flourish. Everything needs renewal, including me.

After the biblical rain comes another limpidly lovely day, and in a fresh outfit of dry, clean clothes, I pull back the black weed-suppressing membrane that covers the top plot. Below my feet is a voyage of discovery. Now is the moment to dig. The first bed will be given over to onions and garlic, which need to get in the ground soon in order to get good and chilly over the winter, which they must do in order to flourish. Not only this day, but other days pass while I dig away at the weakened couch grass and weeds. The couch grass roots need a hard shake as they are the favoured nursery for worms. Back the little wormlets go into the soil. Once the 30 foot by 24 foot area is dug, and every muscle and bone in my body aches, it's time to start adding the digestate. I shovel it into the wheelbarrow, wheel it over to the onion bed, deposit it, return, repeat and repeat. It's exhausting and takes four days to complete, as I can only face doing a bit at a time. Finally, we get to the fun part: digging.

There is a school of thought that says you don't need to dig, the worms will do it for you. And already I have come to subscribe to this method. But, for now, I want to see what lies beneath, and so I dig the digestate in. The good news is that through lying fallow, the top plot has become more fertile. The worms are here. Every fork full turns over between six and a dozen good-sized earthworms. One foot-long worm emerges and I cheer. It's such a relief after the paucity of the bottom plot, when I'd be lucky to find one. Charles Darwin estimated that arable land contains 53,000 worms per acre. Not on my plot. But through inadvertently resting the land, and through feeding the soil, the worm count is on the rise. The worms are my future. If they flourish, I will too. So digging gives me a glimpse into the future, a future made up of connection to the soil, life drawn from it and returning to it. Digging and renewing the soil means that I am changing the nature of this small piece of land. It will no longer be a plot of weeds, it will have a purpose, and next year that purpose will be to grow onions and garlic, perhaps even something else when they have been harvested in the summer. The future beckons to me.

Again, it's a very real metaphor of what God is doing in my life through the act of growing vegetables. Who knew that gardening was so spiritual? But it is. This place enables God to reach me in a way that isn't so easy elsewhere. Everything feels like a metaphor. And I know that, through what I'm doing, I'm seeing his work of renewal leading to flourishing, purpose and, ultimately, a harvest.

It is quiet at the allotments in November. The spring-and-summer-growers have disappeared back to their homes, leaving their plots slumbering over the winter. There is just a hardy crew of us spending our time enriching the soil. Every week seems to bring more tonne bags of digestate, more piles of manure, sacks of leaves collected to make leaf mould.

It is easy to think of a garden, or an allotment, as a place that you inhabit in the summer: sitting outside drinking a glass of white wine, perhaps, taking in the view. But the summer can't happen without the winter. The processes of renewal, restoration, rest and enrichment must all happen now. They are what gives us the high-summer joy. Winter, it turns out, is the real time to garden. This is when the change, the development, the renewal really happens. That's like the rest of life. We want life to be all summer days, sunshine and happiness. Writing this in a pandemic, I know full well that this isn't so. But it is in the seemingly bleak times that renewal happens, that the soil of our own lives can be enriched. It can't be July every month of the year. We need it to be a rainy day in November sometimes, however miserable that experience may be.

There is more soil to be had. My neighbours Richard and Alex have had major work done on their house and garden. Their old floorboards have already created a terrace on the top plot where, hitherto, there was just an unsightly mound. Now, Richard says, would I like some soil? Of course I would. He's offering chalky loam from his back garden, which, due to a redesign, is surplus to requirements. He and I spend two mornings shovelling it into his trailer, driving it round to the allotment and repeating the exercise. This, mixed with the digestate, will fill the raised beds on the top plot and, I hope, be a wonderful growing medium for asparagus, lettuces, broad beans and yet more flowers. There is more barrowing, more shovelling and quite a bit more groaning at the effort required. At the end of it all, the eight raised beds are full of really quite promising soil. The top plot is starting to take shape.

My fleece is back on, plus a jacket, woolly hat, scarf and gloves, and on the last sunny day of the month, I'm back for more barrowing. The joy of going to the allotment on a quiet day is that you see its other residents: the birds. As I walk in, a pair of trotty wagtails are bobbing about on the edge of the ubiquitous puddles in the track. It has to be a hot day in August for there to be no puddles. As I walk further, the twitter of a hedgerow of sparrows behind me, I spot the wave-like flight of a charm of goldfinches ahead. Virtually everyone grows sun-flowers and there are plenty of thistles, so the allotments are goldfinch heaven. But they're shy birds and you won't spot them on a busy Saturday. Take a quiet Friday morning, how-ever, and they will be there. Above, wheeling on the thermals, is a lone red kite. My father would be delighted. At stage left, I can hear the clamour that only comes from starlings, and in and out of the plot come its usual visitors: the blackbirds, robins, pigeons and the neighbourhood black cat. We all co-exist. We are enmeshed together. And what I do now will benefit all of them, with the possible exception of the black cat.

So it begins: hours of shovelling, barrowing and unload-ing. The jacket comes off, then the scarf, hung rakishly on the fence. By the end of the morning, the whole of the bottom plot is thick with digestate. The bottom plot, once so forlorn, looks enriched, like it's been dressed in the finest velvet money can buy. The remaining plants (spinach, chard, kale, purple sprouting broccoli) will all benefit from it. But the real winners are next year's plants, enriched with the forethought and effort of this year – and not a chemical in sight. Next year has to be an even better year, I think to myself, unknowing.

Of course, the soil isn't the only thing to benefit from all this renewal. The simple process of mulching the ground, as our forefathers and mothers have done since time immemorial, renews me too. It takes my view further than the end of the day, the last-minute struggles as we head towards the deadline of the Psalm 23 Garden launch, the office niggles, the commuting exhaustions, the other little (but seemingly large) issues of life. The renewal of the soil says, 'Look beyond today, beyond next year. Remember that this was once sea. Do what you can now to make things better, not just for the land, but for the wildlife and for the people. And then, sit down and let yourself be enriched by the joy of being alive. Life is not all doing. It is not all activity. You should stop now and look.' So I take my flask of tea up to the summerhouse, drink, gaze at the hills beyond the plot, and stop.

DECEMBER

Quiet Times

Stress, pressure and busyness are ratcheting up as we enter December. There are, essentially, only three weeks until we all stop for Christmas, so in every area of life it feels as if There Is Too Much To Be Done.

At work, everyone is frazzled and exhausted. It's been a long year. I'm soldiering on towards my first Chelsea garden, trying to work quickly and well in a fog of unknowing. So often now, my sleep is disturbed by spinning thoughts of the work that needs to be done. I'm in a constant state of writing and rewriting to-do lists, remembering things I'd temporarily forgotten, sitting bolt upright at 3 a.m. and saying things like, 'What about the rock?' or 'Don't forget to fill in that form'. Sometimes it feels as if I'm not sleeping at all.

At home, my mother now needs more support. Here again, I am in a fog of unknowing. My father died having staggered through ten years of dementia. I know what that looks like. My mother's needs are different from his, but because she's from a polite, self-effacing generation, they are hard to express. We are metaphorically playing Pin The Tail On The Donkey as we work out what she needs.

Then there's the pressure of Christmas. Why is Christmas such a pressure? When did the joy get squeezed out of it and replaced by a tsunami of eating, shopping and visiting? Possibly when we – I – lost sight of what was really going on and settled for activity over meaning. Perhaps it's an attempt to blot out meaning, because the meaning of Christmas is so overwhelming. Whatever the cause, there are cards to be written, presents bought and wrapped, a tree to be decorated and enough food made to feed ravening hordes, should they turn up unexpectedly, which they won't. It's not so much Jingle Bells as Jangling Nerves as December gets underway. In the midst of this, therefore, it is wonderful to forge a little bit of time to potter around at the allotment in the quietness. Here, my battered spirit can right itself again. Here, other people's stress and anger can simply slide off me. Here, there is no pressure, as the sky waters the earth and the land rests. Here, the quietness of my surroundings (if you zone out the M3, which I do) seeps into my heart, stilling and quieting it. That's just what I need right now: a place where the tills aren't ringing, the phone isn't pinging, the demands cease and the pressure is off.

And it is quiet. The laughter and chatter of the summer months has gone. The constant-whir-somewhere of a strimmer is silenced. Even the sound of car engines has gone. Few people are here now, and those that do come are on foot or bicycles.

The first day of December dawns clear and bright. The winter sun casts long shadows up the plot. Winter colours of browns, greens, greys and ochres are deep and rich. The starlings' beech trees are majestic against the sky. Allotment holders talk about 'putting their plots to bed for the winter'. Mine might be having a doze, but it's far from somnolent. Lettuces, purple sprouting broccoli, yet more celery, chard, spinach and curly kale are all thriving, with strong, lustrous leaves and vigorous growth.

In the work calendar, December feels like a frazzled end of a linear journey in time, all Secret Santas and deadlines. In the church calendar it is the beginning, as we step, wearily, into Advent and await the much-needed arrival of our saviour. At the allotment, December is a quiet month in a wheel of activity, rather than the straight line of the calendar year. That wheel, that cycle of activity never lets up. It's always time to be planning ahead for something, thinking about what's next, sowing, planting, enriching, imagining the future. So a quiet time is really just the opportunity to breathe, look around you and imagine the future that your little piece of land might have. My future is going to have both more onions and more garlic in it than this year has had. While I was pleased with the 27 onions and the handful of garlic that I harvested in the summer, they didn't go very far. The newly dug bed on the top plot is the site for the onions and garlic to grow. I borrow a scaffolding board from Jim so that I don't compact the soil as I plant, and set to.

The first act is to make 2-inch-deep holes about 6 inches apart the length of the board, on both sides. Then I return to the beginning of the scaffolding board and start dropping in the onion sets, pointy end up, and cover them over with soil. There are to be eight rows of onions, mostly white ones as all-purpose cooking onions, but there really is nothing quite so delicious as a red onion in a summer salad, so two rows of those are added in too. I repeat the trick with the dibber and the scaffolding board until they're all safely in. Then it's the turn of the garlic: three rows, with a clove of garlic dropped into each hole. It is still a wonder to me that a clove of garlic will, in the course of six months, fill itself out and yield a whole bulb of garlic.

In the intervening time, my role with the onions and garlic is marginal. I'm to keep the birds off this area, as they otherwise pull the onion sets and garlic cloves out and eat them; and I'm to water them in dry weather. That's it. Knees, back and legs creak as I stand upright after the planting, my stomach knotted through bending over for so long. I long to sit down, but before I can, the onions and garlic must be protected against the birds.

So I trudge down to the shed, find the 12 shortest bamboo canes and a mass of tangled green netting, and return. The 12 short bamboo canes slip easily into the damp, clay soil. Each one is then topped with an equally small flowerpot. These give the netting something to rest on. Getting the netting untangled and draped correctly over the flowerpots involves frequent knocking off of the flowerpots and quite a bit of muttering.

But in the end, we're there. The netting is pulled tight and then held in place with broken bricks. It won't win any awards, but it will do the job. Furthermore, an area of unproductive, weed-filled claggy clay is now simultaneously being enriched and given its first crop to grow in a goodish while. It's exciting. I retreat to the summerhouse to gaze upon the progress.

The first of the properly cold weather is forecast, so I hang home-made fat balls for the birds in the Victoria plum tree. Joe Robin is the first in, with the starlings watching from the safe distance of the beech trees until I'm a more comfortable distance away.

The greenhouse also needs protection. Tender Mediterranean herbs (tarragon, stevia, lemon verbena) are overwintering in it, and these need protection from the coming cold nights. There are any number of ways to do this. My father used his legendary electrician's skills to rig up a heater using a lightbulb and a car battery. You can light a candle and put it underneath a terracotta flowerpot overnight. I'm opting for a method requiring less skill: wrapping the inside of the greenhouse in bubble wrap. The rise of Amazon has seen more and more deliveries coming to our homes, and much of this involves bubble wrap. I've been bequeathed enough to swathe several greenhouses in it. This is big, fat bubble wrap, not the stress-busting thin type, so surely it will keep the herbs frost-free over the winter.

Wrapping the inside of an eight-sided greenhouse in bubble wrap single-handed is the sort of task that should be included in television competitions. I climb up and down the step ladder, attaching the bubble wrap with plastic twists and wooden clothes pegs. I duck under shelving and skirt round plants. There isn't a hope of me reaching the roof, so the eight sides will have to do. After quite a bit off huffing and puffing the job is done. Just like the onion-and-garlic netting, this won't win any prizes. But if everything survives the winter, I'll be delighted.

The sun is dipping dramatically in the west. The shadows now stretch across the allotment, rather than up it, telling me it's time to think about walking home. I scoop up my wooden trug and pick tonight's meal: celery, lettuce, spinach and chard, all so green that you just know they'll do you good. As I'm about to leave, I bump into a near allotment neighbour who I don't know very well. He's retired and now tends his plot a few yards away. We exchange pleasantries about the weather and how things are growing, indeed simply what's still growing. 'I'm about to dig up some parsnips,' he says. I commend him, not having grown any and having heard horror stories about how difficult they are to germinate. 'You haven't got any parsnips?' he says, incredulously. Obviously, I'm letting the side down here, but I confess that is the truth. 'Well,' he says, 'I've grown four rows. We can't eat any more. I don't know why I grew so many. Help yourself to a row.' A whole row? 'Yes, but do it in the next couple of weeks. I want to mulch the soil,' he says.

I adore parsnips, but I've never had a homegrown one. My father grew potatoes and carrots, but never a parsnip. That was the tradition. So I follow the former businessman down to his plot and there you have it: four long rows of parsnips. 'Grab your spade,' he says, digging. I head back to the shed, pick up my spade and return. He is by now washing the soil off his parsnips, nods and wishes me well. I dig up half a dozen enormous parsnips and conjure up in my mind the soup I'll be making later, thanks entirely to the generosity of a near-stranger. I wipe the soil off the spade, bolt the shed, shut the summerhouse doors, close the greenhouse and bid goodnight to the plot. My shoulders are slightly lower now, my breathing steadier, and my sights are set on the summer (beyond the RHS Chelsea Flower Show), when I'll harvest the onions and garlic, as well as the soup I'll have tonight. Nothing at work could help me achieve this. Not for the first time, I think that allotments should be available on the NHS. And I walk home.

As it turns out, something very like time on the allotment is about to be available on the NHS. In 2020, a £4 million pilot project is launched, which sees doctors able to prescribe patients a walk in the park or a spot of gardening, rather than a packet of pills. The aim is simple: to see if so-called 'green prescriptions' really work. My bet is that the pilot is likely to reveal the unsurprising finding that green prescriptions are absolutely the best thing for some people. NHS Shetland has been issuing 'nature prescriptions' since 2018, sending patients on rambles, out birdwatching and for beach walks. In New Zealand, green prescriptions have been part of medical life for a decade.

Craig Bennett of the Wildlife Trust welcomed the move. He said, 'Through lockdown, millions of people have come to appreciate just how important access to nature is for their physical and mental well-being. It's welcome that the government is moving in this area.'

Among those of us on the allotments, there are plenty battling physical or mental health issues. We are all open about this, which reduces the menace of whatever we're experiencing. People rally round and help those who are less strong, or less able, sick or suffering. This is not, surprisingly, a place for the physically tough and able. It's a place for everyone and all of life's experiences.

At work, there is also something to cheer the spirits. The Queen is our patron, and so earlier in the year, I wrote to the Palace, expressing the hope that we might see the Queen at the RHS Chelsea Flower Show. Truthfully, I never expected to have a response. The Royal Family always attends the Show. The RHS team knows that the Queen is our patron. A plan will doubtless be made very close to the time, and I will not be party to it. But a girl can dream, and my dreams are variously of the Queen and Monty Don on sunny days in May.

'You've got a letter from the Palace,' whispers Jude, who runs our post room. She's hiding behind the door of her domain, beckoning me in, urgently. 'Really?' Ceremoniously, Jude hands the letter over.

I read it. Then I read it again. It is an object lesson in how to write a warm, gracious thank-you letter in three sentences. I shall treasure it for ever. It gets mentioned in dispatches, and colleague's reactions are amazing. Some stand open-mouthed. Others cry, quite genuinely. More laugh with pleasure. And I get a good few hugs.

Under these circumstances, it's helpful to be grounded by the allotment. December is a lull in proceedings. The crazy running around of spring and summer are behind us, and the allotment and I can breathe and take stock. December is beguiling, however. It looks as if nothing is happening, while of course so much is. The renewing, refreshing, replenishing and resting of the land is as important in the cycle of growing as the times when I'm harvesting. Without one you don't have the other. But to my utter amazement, I am still harvesting. I could have harvested every day from May onwards but chose not to, as there are days when I need to eat or process what's come into the house, rather than simply garner more. But I kept a record of what I'd harvested, and in December, we hit Day 95 of note-worthy harvests. This utterly exceeds expectations. And as the purple sprouting broccoli sits waiting for its moment to shine in the spring, there is more to come. It seems unlikely that I will ever buy a supermarket vegetable again (except perhaps the occasional sweet potato), especially now that the little plot has doubled in size.

Remarkably, there are still raspberries on the autumn-fruiting canes and white strawberries sit underneath them. The fruit remains my big passion, and the idea of an actual orchard has not dwindled in my heart. So it's time to add to the tree stock, even though this feels like adding trees rather than creating an orchard. This time last year, I gathered the clans of friends for the planting of apple, greengage and quince trees. This December, on a leaden, grey day, I'm planting alone. The top plot is to have three trees in addition to the fig: a Szechuan pepper, an apricot and a Bramley apple. The latter two will be espaliered in the course of time. The Szechuan pepper is unlikely to grow very large. And the fig has its roots confined so that it doesn't take over entirely.

All four are little more than twigs. It takes a leap of imagination to know that, when I am a very old woman, these will be maturing trees, yielding both fruit and shade, absorbing carbon from the atmosphere, preventing soil erosion with their roots and providing a habitat for wildlife. I lean on my spade and contemplate this, and it makes me smile just as much as the letter from the Palace.

If you've ever found yourself walking in an orchard, or down a drive lined by tall, mature trees, it makes you think of the people who planted them. They were people who knew they'd never see the fulfilment of their dreams. They only knew the saplings, or young trees, but they planted them for generations of people they'd never know, creating a landscape they'd never see, planting for a harvest they'd never eat.

We can all do that. Every garden, no matter how small, can accommodate a tree. And you can have a lot of fun with the choice. That's what I'm doing today. I bought the trees (twigs) from two small, local growers. The fig and apricot are a nod to our warming climate. When I am old, I'll not only wear purple (as the poem says) but hopefully take home baskets of figs and apricots. The Bramley apple links me to my childhood, and the apple orchard at the end of the garden. I adore cooking apples. One tree isn't enough. But it's a start. And the Szechuan pepper is just a recognition that this is my plot and I can do what I want, no matter how eccentric. Research tells me that this tree likes a sunny position (tick) and will have small yellow flowers followed by wonderful pink peppercorns in late summer. I imagine harvesting, drying and using my own peppercorns and feel deliriously smug. Much, much later, I read in Jonathan Drori's beautiful book, *Around The World In 80 Trees*, that the husks around the seeds might not be edible. They cause paraesthesia, a nerve-tricking phenomenon. In this, mint feels cool in the mouth even when it isn't. Chillies make us perceive heat. Szechuan pepper husks make the mouth feel a vibration,

Drori says. 'Within a minute of contact with the spice [those eating it] felt their lips and tongues were buzzing at about 50 times a second. Some people report that it is like licking one's tongue across a 9-volt battery.' How would they know? I surely don't want to. But as I write, the sapling is flourishing, so it's staying, despite the husks.

Just when I think that 11 trees are the limit, another finds me. During the first week of December it is traditional for head gardener Fran's husband, Richard, to take part in a play staged by a village amateur dramatic society. He began doing this an indeterminate number of years ago for the very laudable reason that the idea of being on stage scared him rigid. So he faced his fears, took up amateur dramatics and, of course, utterly loves it.

This Advent sees the performance of *Murder in Play* by Simon Brett. Friends and family descend on the village hall for the performance. I find a seat next to Fran. 'There's a raffle,' she says. 'Have you bought a ticket?' I walk over to the woman holding the box of tickets, separate myself from £1 and return, ticket in hand.

Interestingly, and fatefully, the woman doesn't shake the box of tickets. Instead, she reads out the list of prizes: alcohol of various descriptions, hampers, meals out and so on. But the one that catches my attention is an apple tree. Fran and Richard are donating a local variety of apple: Beau of Beaulieu. 'Oh, I'd like that,' I whisper to Fran. 'You've got enough trees,' she says. She should talk, being head gardener at an arboretum.

Anyway, the raffle lady opens the unshaken box and draws out my ticket. This hasn't happened since I was eight years old and won a box of chocolates in a village raffle, so I'm due a win. Everyone claps politely. 'What prize would you like?' the lady asks. 'I'll have the apple tree, please,' I say. Fran hoots with laughter. And now there are 12.

The apple tree, like its peers on the bottom plot, is already 6 feet tall. Just like its peers it will be espaliered. There is now only one piece of fence-line for it to go along, facing west. That's a good spot. I dig a big hole, slather the roots in mycorrhizal fungi to help it get going, and plant the tree. Twelve fruit trees.

This is the equivalent of an orchard now, even if it doesn't look like it.

Barbara sees what I'm doing and hails me. 'Bill is creating an orchard,' she says. 'Come and see.' Bill, be-hatted and wearing multiple coats, is a long-standing allotment holder, able, friendly, knowledgeable and kind. Somehow, he's been granted a plot to create a proper orchard, not sneaking trees in under the cover of vegetables, and is busy doing it. He's hedged it round with British hedgerow trees. Within that, he's planting 14 fruit and nut trees in serried rows, just like an orchard should be. He gives us the guided tour.

Bill is embodying my dream, a dream that I didn't think was possible, as no new orchards were being grown at the allotments and there are strict rules about the height of trees. Clearly that dream is realizable after all. Barbara is jumping up and down with excitement. This appears to be her dream too. But neither of us needs 14 trees' worth of fruit. 'How would you feel about sharing an orchard plot?' I ask hesitantly. She hugs me and picks me up simultaneously. 'I'd love it,' she says, adding, sotto voce, 'but don't tell Garry. We've got enough to do.'

Bill smiles patiently and goes on digging, while Barbara and I stand at the entrance to the new orchard and plan what we'd plant. This is a fun game, rather like choosing your seven discs for *Desert Island Discs*. It's never the same from one day to the next. Seven trees. What would I plant? Today, I'd choose another cooking apple and another eating apple, a wild cherry plum, a cherry tree (preferably a Bigarreaux), another greengage, a walnut tree for Phil, who loves them, and finally a dessert pear. If it ever happens, depend upon it, that list will be different.

James-the-chairman arrives. Barbara and I are now headily intoxicated with the idea of an orchard and jump up and down some more. 'Please can we put our names down jointly for an orchard plot?' 'You can,' says James. And that's it, the dream of a year ago is now officially registered, very much more likely to become real. A plot where an orchard can be planted may never come up in our lifetimes. But equally, it might, and the prospect of that is quite enough to keep me going. 'We'll make it happen,' says James.

Barbara suggests that, if we're to have an orchard, we should also keep geese and bees. Both she and I are actually a bit nervous about close contact with bees. But here, the motivational force is the idea of honey at the end of the summer. I sign us up for a training day with the local Beekeepers' Association, who are, as my mother would say, 'no more eccentric than is strictly necessary'.

Is my plot smiling? It could well be. There is so much serendipity here. First, the thought of planting an orchard rather than getting married. Then, mentioning it to Maurice at the hairdresser's and suddenly finding myself with an allotment and a couple of trees. A year on, the plot has doubled in size, there are 12 trees (more than enough to qualify as an orchard, even if it doesn't look like an orchard), I'm knee-deep in vegetables and have just put my name down for a proper orchard and keeping bees. Phil is lobbying hard for geese-keeping too. Who knew that life could be altered so unutterably by a little plot of land and the willingness to get up off the sofa?

When I set out on this adventure, I thought that it was about me slowly transforming the plot. And it has been. It's gone from an abandoned wreck without a purpose to a charming, welcoming place, where food actually grows. Of course, it's worked the other way round too. The plot is slowly transforming me. My horizons are broader. I'm willing to try things that daunt me. I'm starting to believe in my own abilities. More than that, I have somewhere to go to decompress after long, busy, stressful days. I have something that isn't work or home and gives in return for what I put in. Perhaps I'm more fruitful too. I'm certainly less constrained and able to see beyond the immediate satisfaction of newspaper bylines and high-profile commissions. They have paled into insignificance alongside tending the soil and producing something that isn't tomorrow's chip paper.

God is like water. He seeps into the cracks we leave for him. That might be through prayer, meditation or mindfulness. It is always when we stop and turn aside from the busyness of life, the clickbait of our phones, the relentless to-do list, that the presence of God can be felt, that his quiet voice can be heard. As I stop at the allotment, as December is quiet, as I am close to nature, it is possible to feel the presence of the creator. There is a stillness, a quietness that I recognize as God's peace. Here, I don't need to strive and struggle to be anything other than I am, and so God can draw alongside. Nothing significant happens in this time. I'm not afforded insights into how to achieve world peace. But my life, my soul, my emotions are stabilized.

The last day of the year is bright and mild, a mirror of the first day. I walk over to the plot to thank it for everything it has meant to me over the past 12 months, to offer up prayers for its future, simply to be with it and part of it, before I'm launched into the craziness of the next year and all that it will bring.

A harvest awaits me on the bottom plot. How it's still doing this is quite extraordinary. Next year, I think, if I plan carefully, I may be able to grow vegetables for the Christmas table. Perhaps parsnips, potatoes and Brussels sprouts (though I can't stand them) could be on my list. There's an ambition.

The top plot is slowly emerging from the weed-suppressing membrane and rejuvenating under inches of mulch. It lacks direction, but that will come, with time. The soil will improve. It will flourish. I know this simply because it's happened with the original plot, and this can give me confidence in stepping forward with the new challenges that the top plot affords.

It's just me and the birds today: the starlings squabbling in the beech trees; the blackbirds hopping into the plot, tilting their heads at me and then going for worms; and the redwings are back in the ivy hedges. I stand next to Beau of Beaulieu thinking about its future, how long it will take to grow into a big, productive tree, what will happen in that intervening time and how my life can now be marked in trees, as some people's are in children and grandchildren. And I feel hope: hope that there will be a future; that I can affect positive change; that positive choices for the world around us can be made and achieve so much. They are big thoughts, so I withdraw to the summerhouse to let them wash over me. When I look back, a robin has flown on to a branch of the raffle prize apple tree and is singing, clear, confident, trilling notes.

We could end here, with a beautiful circle back to the moment that this adventure began. But that would be false. There have been failures: the blackbirds ate my seeds, the pigeons had a good go at lots else, the water butts collapsed on sodden soil. Most of the time, I haven't known what I was doing. I've changed my mind many times. I am not Monty Don. But I think that my heart was in the right place; or at least, if it wasn't, it has become more so. I listened to the soil as it spoke of its need for replenishment. I listened to the trees. I tried hard to listen to my seedlings. And in listening, I became a little bit more in tune with the seasons, with the planet I inhabit. It is no longer wallpaper, a fast-moving, blurred background to my life. I belong. I am rooted. I am trying to make a small contribution to this little plot, and the great comfort is in knowing that it will outlast me, will flourish when I am gone, will yield its harvest to others; that future robins will sit in the trees and sing. And that is enough.

What Happened Next

If this were fiction, I'd now be reflecting on a job well done, on growing more in contact with the seasons, with the earth. I'd be reflecting on the pleasure of living off, through and as part of the land, not seeing it whizz past from a car window. I might even be learning from my plentiful mistakes and looking forward to the year ahead when they could be rectified.

However, we all know what actually happened next: the news reports from China of an illness that seemed terrible but far off; the spread of the coronavirus across the world; a sense of disbelief that it could be coming our way; lockdowns, deaths, working from home (if working at all), closed schools, loneliness, Dominic Cummings, Boris Johnson, more deaths, uncertainty, isolation, clapping, worry, anger, frustration, boredom, an impossible number of deaths, long Covid, grief, loss and fear.

In February, Phil rang and told me that the virus was on the march and that the RHS Chelsea Flower Show wouldn't happen. I didn't want to believe him, but something primal within me knew that he was right. I didn't breathe a word of it at work, where everything was in full swing. We worked flat out, in the hope that the Show would go on. But the inevitable call came in March to say that the Show was off. I had a cough, just a cough, so was at home. A colleague brought my laptop round as the office closed. Total lockdown was declared on 23 March. I felt like Road Runner, running full pelt off a cliff. Hopes, dreams, expectations blown to smithereens.

March is the beginning of the growing season. The greenhouse was full of seedlings. Without the Chelsea Flower Show to worry about, my attention was directed at them. Under the new rules, would it be possible to go to the allotment? Would all that hard work too, come to nought?

Michael Gove is not my idea of what journalists call 'a reliable source'. He strikes me as being a person who is about to spin one line at breakfast time, and then two hours later spin another one. But when he went on breakfast TV on 24 March 2020 to say that allotment holders could keep tending their allotments, I cheered. For once, entirely selectively, I was willing to believe him. The allotment could be tended.

But how? The legal limit for exercise was one hour per day. It takes a lot more than that to look after an allotment, especially in the spring. Geordie and I again teamed up, using our one-hour slots to water each other's greenhouses and keep an eye on seedlings.

In this regard, everything was normal. In all other regards, it wasn't. The main road to the allotment is normally busy, full of traffic all day. Now, I could walk along that road for 15–20 minutes and be passed by one, possibly two cars during that whole time. If someone else was also walking on the pavement, I could walk in the middle of the road to avoid them, and did, frequently. Deer were seen strolling through Winchester High Street regularly. Peregrine falcons nested on the roof of the cathedral. And everywhere there was bird song. The birds were doubtless always there, but finally we could hear them. At the allotments, the endless rumble of the M3 faded to a handful of cars. Every bird at the allotment sang. This is what the world should sound like, I thought.

In that first spring lockdown, everything had been stripped away. My hopes and dreams for the RHS Chelsea Flower Show, the routine of work, commuting, going to church, and my other great passion, horse riding. I couldn't see my friends, and though the street's community was utterly wonderful, I lived a solitary life. Every night I pressed my face against my bedroom window, looking out on to the eerily silent, empty street below and quietly wished its inhabitants goodnight. I still do.

Into that loneliness poured worry – particularly for my mother – fear, helplessness and an overwhelming sense of loss. All that was left was the allotment. It was the one constant in a churning world of anxiety, uncertainty and stress. At the allotment, I still had a purpose and something to do. Conversations could still be had while remaining socially distanced. Food could be grown, tasks undertaken, seasons observed, progress made. To all intents and purposes, things were pretty much the same at the allotment as they had ever been, which in itself was something greatly to be valued. But if anything, they were better: conversations had more value, as did the people with whom you were having them; the natural world seemed more vivid, the bird song louder, the butterflies more plentiful and the milk of human kindness ran all the deeper. Even more significantly, at the allotment I could see the seasons change and time pass, giving me some purchase on where I was in time. All the punctuation marks of the week (the working days, the riding days, Sunday's visit to church) had gone. Days merged into each other. Weeks did too. Easter was cancelled. Then Chelsea. Then summer holidays. Blursday. I was glad of the seasons and the weather to give me something to hold on to.

When Michael Gove gave us all permission to continue tending our plots, there was nothing to be done except head over to the allotment. Work decisions hung in the email ether. By sitting at my desk I could affect no change. So after lunch I walked over to the allotment and pottered about for a couple of hours in the warm sunshine that became the hallmark of the spring of 2020. I weeded the herbaceous border and planted nasturtium seeds, as the plants are great at drawing black fly away from tomatoes. I tidied the greenhouse's messy layers of seedlings and planted achillea, antirrhinum and the last of the broad beans. Outside, I sowed a row of carrots, another of perpetual spinach and harvested last year's perpetual spinach and purple sprouting broccoli. A neighbour had given me a huge box of food for Rufus, my cat. So, in return, I picked her a massive bag of purple sprouting broccoli and left it on her doorstep. Purple sprouting is a plant that rewards patience. Its seedlings grow really quickly; the plant is soon outside and over 3 feet tall; and then it sits there for the best part of a year doing (it would appear) precisely nothing. But once it gets into its stride it produces so much that, to be honest, it becomes a pleasure to give it away in the end, and I'm sure it's a pleasure to receive it, as where would you buy freshly picked PSB?

We were only in the second day of lockdown, but everyone was already helping everyone else: the young and well doing the shopping of the older and infirm, collecting their medical prescriptions, passing on toys to younger children. My contribution was to get the street growing its own food. The 44 houses have the long, thin gardens you'd expect of Victorian terraces. There was time and space to grow. My suggestions of a pumpkin-growing competition for the children, and the provision of squash and courgette plants for the adults, were warmly welcomed. Orders came in. My role was to sow the seeds, care for the seedlings, pot them up and, when the last frosts had passed, give them to their permanent homes. I stood in the potting shed filling pots with compost, and sowing pumpkin, squash, courgette and patty pan seeds. It was a hopeful act for a summer that I couldn't envisage. More than that, it was good to share my new-found enjoyment of growing vegetables. 'Any twit can do it,' I said to myself, and started making little videos to instruct the neighbours in the basics: growing lettuce leaves on a windowsill, runner beans up bamboo canes, potatoes in a plastic sack. Broadcasting chums quickly got in touch to advise me on how to do this very, very much better, or perhaps not do it at all.

It was the most beautiful of springs: mild, sunny, blue-skied. Like the misremembered summers of our childhoods, it never rained. Perhaps spring is always beautiful. But it had been a long time since I noticed it. Now, with the commute gone, I had three extra hours a day to live in. There were no cars, no planes. There was only silence. At first my ears hurt with it. But the birdsong took over. Rufus began waking me at dawn, which grew earlier and earlier, until I was up at 3.50 a.m., sitting in the garden with a cup of tea, listening to the birds establishing the day, watching the sunlight emerge from the end of the garden.

This meant that I could be – and often was – at the allotment very early. As no one was working, everyone was attending to their allotments and the corollary of that was that there was Very Little Water. By mid-April I'd learned to arrive before 7 a.m. to give myself the chance of watering everything.

Don't be fooled. It was not all lyrical beauty and shrewd successes. In fact, it felt as if this was going to be the least productive year on the plot, thanks in part to my lack of knowledge and in part to the birds' busyness. Over the winter, I'd spread the five tonnes of digestate over the whole plot. Dan's former plot, now the top plot, was simply desperate for nourishment. The original bottom plot still needed more help and will do for years. I followed the same method as I'd done for manure, covering layers of cardboard with a thick layer of digestate and assuming that the worms would do their job of incorporating it into the soil. But as I didn't cover everything with black weed-suppressing membrane, the surface was not a snug, warm place for the worms and the digestate remained on the surface, like icing on a cake.

The spring was warm and dry. The digestate dried out. Like an idiot, I sowed my seeds straight into it nonetheless, rather than digging it into the soil below. The serried ranks of allotment birds (pigeons, starlings, blackbirds) had a field day. By mid-May, when everything should have been flourishing, there was instead a scene of devastation. The birds had dug up and eaten all my direct-sown seeds: carrots, spinach, chard, kale and lettuces. They had pulled up my sweet peas to eat the peas. I had sown three lots of chickpeas and had precisely one plant. A late frost killed the kiwi fruit vine and badly set back the grapevine. The Victoria plum tree, which looked frothy and poppety in all its white blossom, was scorched by the frost. There would be no fruit this year. Early-planted potatoes had also been turned brown by the frost, though being tough, it was likely they would recover and shoot again. All six green-sprouting broccoli plants that Geordie gave me died. I felt like a complete and utter failure and couldn't see how there would be anything to eat this year, except the beans and tomatoes waiting in the safety of the greenhouse. Even the tomatoes seemed like a failure. Mine were one and a half inches tall. Monty Don's tomatoes on *Gardeners' World* were a foot tall. It felt like a desperate addition to a desperate spring. Despair gripped my heart. I wanted to give up. Who did I think I was, trying to tell other novices how to grow vegetables? Why did I think that I could tend an allotment? Clearly, not every twit can do it. Certainly not me.

But then, as I was seriously considering handing back the keys, something wonderful happened to stop me giving up. Before lockdown, before we knew that there would even be a pandemic, my good friend and neighbour Angela had asked me if I wanted her greenhouse. She was re-landscaping the end of her garden and had no further need of it. With no disrespect to the little greenhouse, this is a proper grown-up greenhouse, 8 feet by 10 feet, with a door that actually closes, and a window that opens. It is all mod cons.

Before lockdown, Angela and I dismantled it, and I paid someone to build a sound foundation for it at the allotment. I ferried the dismantled metal structure over to the plot. Then lockdown came and with it a sense of helplessness. I didn't feel equal to the task of constructing a greenhouse alone. However, in mid-April I arrived at the allotment to see the frame of the greenhouse standing firm and complete. The Allotment Faeries, unable to bear seeing a job left undone, had simply put it up for me overnight. I wept with joy. Perhaps it would be possible to continue after all. I wasn't as alone as I felt.

Now, a world of possibility opened up before me. Angela left all the glass outside her house, and for two days I drove backwards and forwards to the allotment with it, hoping very sincerely that I wouldn't meet a policeman. Geordie and I glazed it on a burningly hot spring day. Believe me when I say that glazing a greenhouse and remaining socially distanced is quite a challenge, but we did it.

The big greenhouse became a totem for hope, rebirth, flourishing, sharing (Geordie's seedlings lived in there too) and the unexpected. It refocused my mind from the bird-induced carnage outside and gave the tomatoes somewhere bird-free to live. Among them were beef tomatoes, one of which, hiding behind leaves, grew to the size of both of my hands. They were the most delicious tomatoes I'd ever eaten.

All of life was in that spring at the allotment: hope, despair, community, sickness, death, failure, success, stability, uncertainty, beauty and, more than that, a sense that this would continue whether or not I survived the coronavirus. At a time when we all became aware of our own mortality, I realized that the plot would outlast me, and that was a comfort.

During the summer, I learnt the very valuable lesson of 'enough' in far more depth than I had in the first year. It took the broad beans, peas and chickpeas several sowings before the birds gave up and I finally had plants. But everything that waited for longer in the little greenhouse before heading outside missed the feathered onslaught and was flourishing. On the bottom plot there were six varieties of climbing bean, a similar number of lettuce (including my favourite, lollo rosso), sweetcorn and, happily, chard and spinach.

On the day that Dominic Cummings made his 'I'm not sorry' speech, I threw the drying-up towel at the radio and decided the only course of action was to buy seedlings. Yvonne's Plants was run by the eponymous nurserywoman in a nearby village. She sold at the farmers' markets. I rang her. Did she have chard and spinach? She'd had exactly the same problem with blackbirds, she said, making me feel a whole lot less stupid. Yes, she could deliver. But could I put in a bigger order to make it worth the trip? I asked around the street, as half the houses were now growing vegetables. Dozens ordered flowering plants, strawberry plants, herbs and pots and pots of vegetable seedlings. Yvonne delivered. I had massively overordered both spinach and chard, and instead of having just one row of each, which would have been enough, I had entire beds of both, enough to feed myself, friends, neighbours, and quite possibly the other half of the street who weren't growing anything.

I also overdid it on the tomatoes. There are, after all, so many lovely varieties to try. I didn't expect all my seeds to flourish, and it took them a long time to do so. But in the end, they did. I had 26 tomato plants. As the plot had doubled in size, there was room for them all, and in the depths of winter I'm still eating home-made tomato soup, the taste of summer drawn from the freezer.

I went to the allotment before work and after work. Focusing on taking the Psalm 23 Garden to Chelsea the following year kept our team going. But the weight of uncertainty about whether the RHS Chelsea Flower Show would happen in 2021 was often crushing for me. Working in isolation was hard. I missed the team bouncing ideas off each other and the ability to walk over to a colleague's desk and say, 'Have you got a minute?' Sometimes it was a joy, sometimes a burden, always the best thing I'd ever done and sometimes, fearfully, a thing that no one would ever see or appreciate. I'm generally quiet and self-effacing, but this felt like a piece of work that needed to be seen; it felt like a psalm for a pandemic. I was a high-wire act without a net.

Very often, going to the allotment was the only thing that calmed me. The very basic life-giving acts of watering, weeding and harvesting restored some kind of order to my shattered spirit. Scientific studies over the summer showed that those who gardened generally saw their mental health improve. I can testify to that. But it was a daily struggle. Real gardening is very different from what you see on the TV.

One day at the end of June saw some difficult work conversations. The hard thing about working alone is that you have no one to turn to on the next desk and say, 'Honestly, what did you think about that?' It stays with you. So I walked over the hill to the allotment and thought about the future. It was invisible and uncertain, but I could keep growing. I'd harvested the onions and garlic and so had a big space into which I could plant late-yielding plants. Three uchiki kuri squash would do the job. They sound exotic, but they are in fact orange-coloured, fat, tear-drop-shaped squash that are sublimely sweet. I hoed round the leeks, which were just pencil-sized at this stage, and watered the small greenhouse.

On my way out, I spotted two abandoned tomato plants that were on the point of death. They were obviously superfluous to someone else's requirements and had been left in the general dumping area, their soil dried out, their attenuated stems thin, their leaves starting to turn yellow. I was tired and all for going home, but I couldn't walk past them. They'd got this far, surely they deserved the chance to flourish? 'Come on then,' I said, 'let's get you planted.' Mercifully, there was a little space in one of the many areas given over to tomatoes, certainly enough room for these two little tragic plants. I gave them a stake each to grow up, tied them in, watered and fed them, and uttered a prayer. May they flourish and thrive and reach their potential, and may I, may the Psalm 23 Garden. Please don't let all this trying, all this hard work come to nothing.

One of the main points of the Psalm 23 Garden was to inspire communities to create their own gardens on its theme. Imagine all those lovely spaces redeemed from not very much by local people. Imagine what could happen. By late summer it was possible to head out and film again. James, cameraman Alex and I headed to the pilot project for this at a church in north Hampshire. Built in the 1960s, the church had a large area of featureless grass, but also a vicar with the vision to change it. The first Psalm 23-inspired garden was born and created by just three people in the first lockdown. It featured a wildflower labyrinth and tree stumps to sit on.

We spent the whole day filming and interviewing. Locals spoke movingly about the spiritual, mental and emotional sustenance they drew from the garden. The hands-on-gardener's voice cracked as he said it had kept him sane during lockdown. The vicar talked about a future that the garden could give that no one could envisage. The possibilities were endless. An idea drawn up at my desk was impacting lives, and that doesn't often happen to me. It was uplifting, hope-giving and inspiring. Seeing it made me all the more determined to keep going, and to channel my energies into the allotment too. If three people could make a garden during lockdown, I could carry on despite the forces of frosts, birds, slugs, lack of water and an overwhelming lack of experience.

By high summer, the herbaceous border and the two raised beds on the top plot were vivid with colour. No one had been able to buy seeds in the spring, so it had simply been a case of planting what you had. What I had was clashing colours: shocking pink cosmos, red snapdragons, the orange-coloured tithonia Red Torch and yellow dill. They all grew together in a riot of colour. Thank goodness Sarah Eberle couldn't see it. But it did make everyone smile. And it was constantly a-buzz with bees. Bumble bees slept in the eyes of the tithonia, and the air was full of the sound of the droning, thrum-thrumming of many different sorts of bee.

Then Sarah Eberle did see it. We were still having monthly meetings, to keep the project on track. Tradition dictated that I drove to her house and that we sat outside on benches several metres apart. 'Would you like to come to me for a change?' I said. 'We could go to the allotment.'

As she drove through the gates, she called out of the window, 'I love it. I love it already.' It was the longest meeting we ever had because it took so long even to start. First, she wanted to see all around and was introduced to many of my friends.

Then she wanted to see the fields, the sheep, the hens, the geese and pigs. Finally, we turned back to my plot. Standing at the entrance in the manner of a Chelsea Flower Show judge, she said, 'Shall I get my clipboard out?' and laughed. Relief swept over me. I'd spent much of the previous two days weeding, watering, telling the tomatoes to stand up straight, really genuinely worried about what a world-class designer would make of the little plot. But of course, Sarah was generous with her praise, gave advice and took home a massive box of vegetables for her pains. I've no idea what we talked about in the meeting, but she didn't laugh at the mix of orange, red, yellow and pink flowers. She deserves a gold medal for that.

During the summer there was also Enough to Eat. In fact, there was more than enough. Far more. Courgettes, beans, tomatoes, lettuce, all were given away to strangers in the street, who then morphed into neighbours with names, lives, families, stories to tell, struggles, hopes and fears. On one memorable day, the big greenhouse yielded eight cucumbers, seven more than I could eat. I left them on neighbours' doorsteps. Cucumbers seem to flourish on slowly improving clay soil.

In September, the summerhouse gained a new role: the place to store squashes and pumpkins. There were a dozen butternut squash, a handful of uchiki kuri, three or four spaghetti squash and 13 pumpkins. More than enough again, so I started giving them away. I carried on giving them away. But there is still plenty to get me through the winter. Why did I doubt that it would be otherwise?

Winter came and with it more lockdowns, more restrictions. New strains of the virus were found, numbers rose alarmingly, people grieved, and with this came an incipient sense of despair. Had we not done enough? Had we not suffered sufficiently? Was there no end in sight? There wasn't. I started to fear that all the work on the Psalm 23 Garden was again in jeopardy, and only you will know whether it was, as by the time you read this, the RHS Chelsea Flower Show will either have happened or not. Now, the uncertainty gnaws at me, frets me, stops me sleeping. It is hard enough to do a world-class piece of work on a global stage at the best of times, but doing it repeatedly in a pandemic with no sense of whether you'll ever see the garden built, the story told, or not, has been an immense struggle.

What to do? I rang tree surgeon Mark Merritt and ordered a lorryload of woodchip. The top plot needed to take shape and that meant making paths and that meant woodchip. One cold, frosty morning just before Christmas, Mark's colleague Andy arrived at the allotment, youthful, wind-tanned, cheerful, smiling. He emptied the lorryload of woodchip next to the top plot and headed off. It was, seasonally appropriately enough, a fir tree that had been felled, and the steaming mound smelt like a giant air freshener.

Over the course of three days, I shovelled and barrowed the woodchip up and down the plot, first making paths at the top, giving it a sense of cohesion that it simply hadn't had before. Then I turned my attention to the terrace in front of the summerhouse. For a whole year it had simply been covered in black weed-suppressing membrane. It looked and felt unloved and unfinished. Under a bright blue, clear winter's sky, I spent three hours layering it up with woodchip and at the end I could convince myself that it looked mighty fine, certainly better, and definitely a long way from the pointless mound of soil that Dan had in the corner of the plot. Now it had a purpose and looked like something, instead of nothing. An extended Christmas was cancelled. So, on Boxing Day, I walked over to the plot. There was nothing else to do. I was the only person there, but not the only creature. Above me, two red kites were quartering the allotments looking for prey. Red kites mostly eat carrion and roadkill, but they'll sometimes take voles, mice and birds, so the small allotment birds were a-hush as these mighty birds of prey flew overhead.

How glad my father would have been to have seen them. It was the least I could do to turn from my path-making endeavours and stand and watch. 'Hello,' I said, with no one around to scoff at me for talking to birds, 'I'm glad to see you. There are rats.' The red kites wheeled and soared, entirely indifferent to me. I stood and gazed, entirely captivated by them. One, glad that there weren't any humans around for a change, wheeled down to just 20 feet above me. It flew on towards the gate and then disappeared from view, dropping down; the end of something, but continued life for the red kite. All this the allotment gave me, before I'd even turned the key in the lock of the shed, picked up my shovel and worked: a connection with my long-dead father, a sense of being part of the world, but insignificant, the ability to look up, not down, to see the dreamed-of future that my father had, fulfilled; to know I am planting for someone else really, and I hope they appreciate it.

During the pandemic, the allotment kept me both sane and fed. It gave me a focus. Everything around me was entirely out of my control. That's a terrible feeling, being flotsam and jetsam in your own life, bobbing like a cork on the sea. So I appreciated the tangible tasks that the allotment afforded, weeding, sowing, pricking out, planting, watering, more watering, more planting, and suddenly harvesting and cooking, the summer over before it had begun, and mulching and manuring coming round more quickly than I could have imagined. When I could not affect change with the RHS Chelsea Flower Show, I planted. When I couldn't communicate effectively, I weeded. When I ran out of ways to help my mother, I watered.

And it wasn't just me. All of us did, and we talked about it too. We talked about our fears, our struggles, our worries and concerns, our health and finances. Sharing them made them less frightening. Some of our number contracted the coronavirus. Others were bereaved. Others lost their work. In among it, there was a feeling of solidarity.

Sensing this, lots of people applied for plots. This has been true across the country as waiting lists lengthen. Ours lengthened too. People knew intuitively that having an allotment would be good for their physical and mental health. They had an inkling that it was about more than growing food. Autumn is when we renew our commitment to our plots, signing up for another year, paying our fees. When spaces became available, new faces appeared, people with inappropriate shoes, whose clothes were far too smart and clean for the digging, weeding and, in some cases, clearance work that they'd be doing.

Often, James-the-chairman would wander over to my plot

to introduce me to new people. I was, it seemed, the poster child of what was possible with a bit of hard graft, even though I'd known absolutely nothing. He didn't need to say, 'Hazel hadn't a clue what she was doing, but look at this,' because I took the cue and said it for him. There were lots of relieved faces, but some daunted ones too: 'You did this by yourself? I could never do that.' Actually, I did it with the help of a community, some on the plot, some not. I fed people I don't know as well as those I do. I sent seed to friends around the country and got people growing in their gardens, as well as along the street. I fed myself. I got fitter. I stayed relatively sane. 'Honestly,' I say to all the new faces, 'you can do it and you will. You'll do it your own way, and in doing it, you'll find that your little bit of land gives you back far more than you could have imagined.'

'What will it give me?' they say. 'You'll have to wait and see,' I say, inscrutably. But it's true. By labouring, by working for my food, I have appreciated it so much more. By growing my own, I have grown enough for others. By being connected to the earth, I have heard its cries and am doing what I can to help it. By working year-round, I am in touch with the weather and the seasons. But I am just passing through, as the sea sponge tells me. I am here for now and would like to make a positive difference. And when I'm gone, someone else can flourish here, pick the fruit, sit in the summerhouse and gaze at the red kites.

Just a little bit of me will be left behind. I commissioned a local blacksmith to make a weathervane for the shed during the first lockdown. It features me digging, accompanied by Rufus the cat. So Rufus and I will be telling the wind direction long after anyone can remember who we were. And hopefully, the robin will still be singing its clear, trilling song in the branches of the trees. It has more to choose from now.

Appendix

Having an allotment isn't really about growing vegetables, it's about growing yourself, growing relationships and caring for a little plot of land. If that sounds like it could be for you, what should you do next?

You can apply for an allotment at www.gov.uk/apply-allotment, and you can find out more about allotments and how to care for yours from the National Allotment Society (nsalg.org.uk). You may be on a waiting list for a while, but an allotment will come up eventually.

But you don't need an allotment to grow vegetables and fruit. You could turn over a little bit of your back garden for this, plant fruit trees, or if you live in a flat, simply grow herbs on a windowsill. Or you could ask your local council if it's possible to grow on untended land. Finally, you could team up with someone who's got a garden and needs a bit of help or has space to share by visiting landshare.net. Whichever way you choose to grow, it's all wonderful.

It's always handy to have advice from someone who's done this before you. The best advice will come from neighbours or friends with similar soil. You can learn from their successes and their failures. There are plenty of internet allotment groups, but I'd caution against these as the advice will come from around the country and won't be pertinent to your area. Seek local advice.

After that, listen to those who do this for a living. In the growing season (March–September), it is a ritual for me to watch *Gardeners' World* and listen to the advice of Monty Don, Carol Klein and Joe Swift. Magazines like *Gardeners' World Magazine* and *Grow Your Own* give you regular to-do lists, so you know what you should be doing, if you could ever get up off the sofa.

If I were to advise you to learn from one person, however, it would be Charles Dowding, whose no-dig approach to gardening will save your back and improve your soil simultaneously. You can read his books, follow his website (www.charlesdowding.co.uk) or watch him on YouTube.

After all of that, there are some great books to read, which may really inspire you. For me, gardening books are rather like cookery books, inspiring and only sometimes referred to. That doesn't stop me buying more of both. Here are my top ten suggestions:

1 *RHS Allotment Journal*: this gives you handy tips of what to do month by month, and space to write down what you achieved each week.
2 *Allotment Month By Month*, by Alan Buckingham: a really handy run-through of what to sow, plant and harvest every month. A vital book for anyone wanting to grow fruit or vegetables, no matter where they do it.
3 *Square Foot Gardening*, by Mel Bartholomew: an ideal starter book if your space is very limited.
4 *Jekka's Complete Herb Book*, by Jekka McVicar: the queen of herbs tells you how to grow all manner of them (including ones you may never have heard of) and what gorgeous produce to make from them. This can be inspiring if you only have a windowsill or balcony.
5 *Creating Your Own Back Garden Nature Reserve*, by Chris Packham: this book helps us to remember that any gardening endeavour is a shared space with the rest of nature.

It helps you identify and cater for the flora and fauna that will enrich your garden or allotment, as well as the planet and your life.

6 *Organic Gardening*, by John Fedor: this book will help you never buy any chemicals or pesticides again, and see your plants flourish.

7 *Companion Planting*, by Richard Bird: some plants help deter pests. Knowing what to plant where can be really helpful to the vegetable gardener, and this book is a great introduction.

8 *Gardening on Clay*, by Peter Jones: when I was stuck not knowing how to cope with clay after a lifetime on chalk, this was a very handy resource.

9 *Bob Flowerdew's Complete Fruit Book*: it's described as the 'definitive sourcebook to growing, harvesting and cooking fruit', and it is.

10 *Cherries* by Norman H. Grubb: essentially, this is just a list, but an inspiring one, of all the cherry trees that you might grow. If you can grow one, do. You'll never regret it.

And if all of this seems like a far-off impossibility, my commissioning editor says to tell you to just try growing some cress in a saucer. But honestly, you can do more than that. Buy some seeds and give it a try.

Recipes

If you do end up growing some plants, here are a few of my favourite allotment recipes for you to try.

Courgette Cake

2 large eggs
8 g soft brown sugar
1 tsp vanilla
2 tsp cinnamon
½ tsp baking powder
140 g sultanas or raisins
120 ml British rape seed oil
350 g grated courgette
300 g plain flower
¼ tsp nutmeg
85 g chopped walnuts, or other nuts

Mix all the ingredients together. Put in a lined loaf tin. Cook at Gas Mark 4 for 1 hour. Stand on a rack to cool. Serve sliced, with butter.

Elderberry Cordial

Elderberries still on their stalks
Granulated sugar
11 cloves
2 cm peeled, sliced ginger
The juice of 1 orange or lemon

Place the elderberries, still on their umbrella-like stalks, in a large pan and cover with water. Bring to the boil, cover and simmer for 20 minutes.

Leave to cool and strain through a jelly bag, or a clean drying-up towel. Allow this to hang overnight. Avoid the temptation of squeezing the bag. If you do, you'll get cloudy liquid.

Compost the pulp. Measure the liquid and pour into a clean pan. For each litre of juice add 500 g of granulated sugar, the cloves, ginger and citrus juice. Bring to the boil, reduce the heat and simmer for 10 minutes, stirring until the sugar is dissolved.

Sieve to remove the spices. Pour the cordial into heated bottles, leaving 2.5 cm at the top. Seal. The cordial lasts for two years in a cool, dark place. Once opened, keep in the fridge.

Fresh chickpea hummus

1 lb fresh chickpeas weighed in their pods
2 tbsp tahini
½ tsp salt
2 tbsp water
2 tbsp British rape seed oil
1 garlic clove
Lemon juice

Remove the chickpeas from their pods. Steam them for 20 minutes. Remove from the water and splash with cold water. Cool for an hour. Blend with the other ingredients, adding more water or rape seed oil if the mixture is too firm.